SANDRINGHAM,

PAST AND PRESENT.

With Twelve Illustrations of the Neighbourhood.

BY

MRS. HERBERT JONES.

London:

JARROLD & SONS, 3, PATERNOSTER BUILDINGS.
1888.

PREFACE.

The following pages, containing some particulars of the present aspect and past history of Sandringham, are mainly reprinted from "Sandringham, Past and Present," as it appeared in 1883. The present volume is published with additions and alterations.

C. R. J.

Sculthorpe,
  Norfolk,
    December, 1887.

TABLE OF CONTENTS.

ILLUSTRATIONS.

Sandringham, Past and Present.

CHAPTER I.

ACQUISITION OF SANDRINGHAM — SCENERY — DEER PARK—SHOOTING.

THERE is a spot in Norfolk which claims notice and memorial, for other reasons even than the one which has given it, in these later years, so strong and unique an interest in the thoughts and heart of England.

The Past of Sandringham,—in which, although the dust of centuries has thickened over it, details and incidents of historical value can be discerned—forms a full and rich background to the vivid Present now lighting up, with a brilliant modern life, this favoured corner of our land.

A description of some points in the existing aspect of Sandringham, with allusion, where necessary, to previous times, will occupy the first part of the following sketch, while some particulars of its earlier owners will be furnished afterwards, to give the subject its due and just associations.

The place was purchased in 1861 as a shooting-box for the Prince of Wales; but Lord Palmerston, who intimated to the Prince Consort Mr. Spencer Cowper's willingness to part with Sandringham, and furnished the information which determined the selection, sagaciously foresaw in it the materials for a complete and attractive country seat, so situated as to be especially free from harassing or unwelcome circumstances.

It now not only affords pheasant shooting and partridge driving of the first order, besides abounding with woodcock, snipe, and sea-fowl, but has developed gradually into a convenient home, and holds up a note-worthy example of what can be done to improve an estate, and to raise to a high standard of excellence the cultivation of its land, the construction of its roads, the character of its cottages and farm premises, the quality of its stock, the disposition of trees in its woods and plantations, and, above all, the condition, physical and mental, of its inhabitants.

Sandringham, which is also the centre of a generous local hospitality, has not only been in every way raised, benefited, and enriched since it passed into the royal hands which may be said to have created it afresh, but rests under the happy glow shed over it by the preference of a princess,

"Whose peerless feature joinèd with her birth,
Approves her fit for none but for a king."

Shakespeare's "HENRY VI."
Part I., act v., *scene* 5.

The Norfolk residence of the Prince of Wales stands between three and four miles

from the sea; south of it lie the parishes of
West Newton, Appleton, and Babingley, and
between it and the sea, Sandringham Warren
and the village, woods, and hills of Wolferton.* Wolferton borders on the Wash, at a
spot about seven miles from King's Lynn.

This ground was well protected in Roman
days; at Brancaster, at the north-west corner
of Norfolk, a strong fortress mounted guard
over the entrance of the Wash, and at Rising,
a Roman defence existed in the huge circular
ridges overlooking the sea, where the castle
was afterwards placed.

A chain of hills runs from north to south
between the village of Wolferton and Sandringham; they rise above the marshy margin
of the sea, glowing with amber moss and
purple heather, with a view over the sea of
the distant spire of Boston Church, on the
Lincolnshire coast; commanding on one side

---

* These five parishes, with a part of Dersingham,
constitute the estate, which amounts altogether to some
eight thousand acres.

the rich marsh-meadows dotted with cattle, and shining with afternoon sun-streaks, after the manner of Paul Potter; and on the other the wild and picturesque heath which is broken by the plantations of Sandringham.

Standing on "Sandringham Heights," at a point where a cottage and belle-vue have been placed on a plateau, and looking towards the sea, Snettisham Church is seen far to the right; Ken Hill, a wooded promontory near it, shows its dark ridge above the pastures; an undulating tract of heath shuts the green expanse in on the left, while, close in front, plantations on the western slope clothe the foreground. Sea, heath, hill, and woodland combine with the soil under cultivation, and the well-ordered and well-conditioned villages, to give this estate the charm of variety, which, it must be acknowledged, is also not wanting to the climate.

The deer which, after the gates have closed upon this pleasant scenery, are to be seen feeding in the glades of the park, and enlivening with their graceful movements the shadows of the beeches and oaks scattered about, are not the first which have stocked a royal deer park in this neighbourhood, or even on this estate.

Castle Rising Chace, the only royal deer park existing in mediæval days in Norfolk, extended to "Babingley Mill," and West Newton. To revert for a moment to those earlier days :—

John Vere, Earl of Oxford, the owner of Sandringham, was Ranger of the Chace early in the reign of Henry VII.

In 1545, Henry VIII. parted with the Chace and Castle Manor to Thomas Howard, Duke of Norfolk, in exchange for some manors in Suffolk, belonging to the latter.

The boundaries of the deer park are defined by some evidence given by an old peasant, who had lived most of his life at Castle Rising, before the magistrates of Lynn, on the 26th of July, 1597.

" John Jeffrey, of Rising Castle, labourer,

aged seventy-six, then deposed that he had known Rising Chace sixty years ; and boundeth the limits, purlieus, or walks of the Chace thus :—' From Rysinge to Babingley Mill, from thence to Ratleman's Lane, so to Hall Lane, so to Butler's Cross, so in a green way leading to Newton, &c., &c.' "

The depositions were taken in consequence of a dispute which had arisen about the bounds of the Chace between William Cobbe, of Sandringham, and the widowed Countess of Arundel.

The deposition of the old man agrees with a description of the Chace written eight years previously, in 1589, when the Earl of Arundel, who then possessed Castle Rising, was attainted, and a survey of his property made by a special commission.

If the southern part of what is now the Prince of Wales's estate was thus inhabited by deer, the northern part was overrun by sheep. Dersingham was a tract covered with ling, brushwood, and short grasses, where large flocks of sheep wandered and browsed.

In 1575, Christopher Walpole, of Anmer Hall, bought 180 acres of land in Dersingham, besides a "foldcourse," called Eastling Course. Much of the eastern part of the parish (adjoining Bircham) was not enclosed until towards the end of the last century, and had been only used previously for sheepwalk or foldcourse; this formed a portion of the land which was sold by the late Marquis of Cholmondeley, the representative of the Walpoles, to Mr. Motteux, of Sandringham; it now forms part of the royal demesne.

Dersingham, then as now, had its sandy heath and lonely footpaths leading towards the village, which, from the fourteenth century, has been crowned by a church remarkable for size and beauty. Wild birds flew in flocks over the sea-flanked district; the great bustard, which has ceased to breed in Norfolk for more than forty years, crouched among the corn, or winged its way to headquarters,—

" Vainly the fowler's eye
   Might mark thy distant flight to do thee wrong,
 As, darkly painted on the crimson sky,
   Thy figure floats along ; "

or, rising slowly in numbers, as a dark cloud,
startled the solitary peasant on his homeward
way.

The huge, noble birds, as big as overgrown
turkeys, were known in this neighbourhood in
the present century, and even longer ago than
1527, when a bustard is mentioned in the
Hunstanton Hall Privy Purse Accounts as
" kylled with ye crosbowe on Wedynsday."
Such a bird would afford a fine meal ; one
which was shot at Westacre, their principal Norfolk haunt, in 1820, weighed twenty-
eight pounds. The " drove," as it was called,
at Westacre consisted at that time of nineteen
or twenty birds.

But a much earlier notice of the Norfolk
bustard than even that in the account-book
at Hunstanton, exists in the Lynn Chamber-
lains' Accounts, which are among the Cor-
poration documents. In 1371, " the 44th of

Edward III.," 39*s.* 8*d.* was paid "for wine, bustards, herons, and oats, presented to John Nevile, Admiral."

They could, however, scarcely have been very common then, for in the repeated lists of food sent to Queen Isabella at Castle Rising, they are never mentioned; nor did they form a dish at a grand dinner given at Lynn to the Lord Chancellor of England in Henry the Fourth's time, at which curlew, duck, plover, and other local delicacies abounded. But as this dinner was eaten on St. Katharine's Day, which is in November, the omission may perhaps go to prove that the bustard migrated from September to Christmas. In February, 1838, a bustard was sold at Cambridge, which, it was ascertained, had been killed at Dersingham.* This Dersingham bird was the last of a group of seven which had been observed at Hillington, not

* Several fine specimens of the Great and Little Bustard, caught in Norfolk, are to be seen in the Norfolk and Norwich Museum.

far off, and which soon dwindled down to
three. Agricultural progress, especially the
introduction of the horse hoe, and the practice
of covering ground with plantations, interfered
with their habits, and gradually drove these
shy, grand birds from the tracts where they
had flourished so long. Good as they were
to eat, it came to be beef or bustards, and
the turnips carried the day.

But although the bustards have vanished,
the fact remains that one of the chief features
of the Sandringham estate is the excellent
capability it affords for sport of almost every
sort and description. The coverts are abun-
dantly stocked with game, and the land is
particularly suitable for partridges. The
Prince of Wales, being a keen sportsman,
takes the chief management of the shooting
into his own hands, and no day's sport is
ever better arranged than it is upon the
Sandringham estate.

There is always an early start for a day's
partridge driving. The guns having previ-

ously drawn the numbers for their places, change in routine throughout the day, thus ensuring that no one gun should have a better chance than another.

The army of beaters, usually between fifty and sixty in number, are all dressed alike in blue blouses, with a red badge and number, black chimney hats with a red ribbon, and each beater, when partridge driving, carries a flag. Looking round, it might almost be imagined that a large band of French peasants were scouring the country in extended order. The army divides, and sweeps the country under the command of the head keeper (who is mounted), driving the partridges over the guns.

The coverts are beautifully kept, and well adapted to show game—Wolferton Wood is by far the finest of them, and the most picturesque. It is supposed to have extended along the coast, in times gone by, until it joined Riffley Wood, the property of Sir William ffolkes, near Lynn. Certainly the

woods bear a strong resemblance to one
another, with their ancient gnarled oaks, their
tangled underwood, and brakes.

Wolferton Wood is the "biggest day" on
the estate. The same army of beaters appears in the same uniform, and they do their
work quietly and effectually. A tent is pitched
for luncheon, which is generally graced by the
presence of the Princess of Wales, the Prin-
cesses, and any ladies who may be staying at
Sandringham, Her Royal Highness invariably
taking a great interest in the sport.

The shooting at Sandringham is always
made a pleasure, not a toil, and anyone who
has had the honour of receiving an invitation
to shoot, can testify that the Prince of Wales
is not only the most courteous and genial of
hosts, but also one of the keenest and most
unselfish of sportsmen.

CHAPTER II.

FLORA——ENTRANCE TO SANDRINGHAM——GARDEN
——HOUSE,

HE heath ground of Dersingham
and Sandringham forms one
only of the many natural features of the Sandringham estate,
on which, from the variety of soils,
and the diverse character of the situ-
ations it includes, a rich and manifold
plant life necessarily abounds.

The salt marshes at Wolferton, the river
at Babingley, the sandy or muddy sea-shore,
the heath, the peaty fen, the pastures, woods,
and meadows, severally produce and nourish
their appropriate species of those wild flower-
ing plants, whose minute germs are, according
to the aspect in which they are viewed, " the

stinking violets that spoil the scent" for the
sportsman, the weeds which harass the farmer,
the specimens which delight the botanist, or
the "joy for ever" of the lover of nature.
Some of these deck profusely the hoary wall,
the grassy roadside, or the ruined fragment
of masonry.

On the churchyard wall at Sandringham
wave the soft grey tufts of the crested hair-
grass, and the little wall-speedwell shows its
turquoise eye; the porch of Babingley is en-
crusted with the sticky, clinging leaves of the
hairy rock-cress ; the yellow archangel* shines
softly under the hedges ; the blue-bell covers
with a mundane sky the floor of Wolferton
wood, where the air is sweet with lily-of-the
valley, and the dim shade lighted by its bells;
the rosy campion and velvet foxglove speckle
the fields ; the horned poppy looks out to sea,
and by its side the sand is laced over by the
tendrils of the faintly-tinted sea-side convol-

* *Galeobdolon luteum.*

vulus; the marsh-marigold burns in the glassy pool; the buckbean covers the marsh with a fringed and piled web of pink and white; grand masses of gorse and broom flower together in bold and fragrant glory on the broken ground where the white main road cuts the heath; the erica, which wraps its warm, bright tint over the hills in August, is scarcely less beautiful in March, when the flying clouds toss their shadows about the thick deep network, and turn it to the richest sable.

At Dersingham the pink petals of the cranberry promise a harvest of piquant fruit; and in the plantations, which shelter and embellish the roads as they come gradually near to the house at Sandringham, the bird-cherry and wild crab peep out from behind the firs, and cross the silver stems of the birch-trees.

Three drives meet where these plantations run up to the main entrance gate, leading from east, west, and north.

The principal gate by which Sandringham

is entered is a fine specimen of modern
wrought iron, so delicately elaborated by the
skilful handicraftsmen of Norwich into sprays,
flowers, and fruitful vines, that the dark, dull
tint of the iron seems to implore some touch
of happier colour. It opens on to an avenue
of large limes, ending at, but not faced by,
the house. This avenue has the unusual
charm of being part of the garden or pleasure-
ground, not of the park ; the broad drive
between the limes approaches the north side
of the house, the right-hand trees leading up
to the north-east corner. The drive continues
straight on until it reaches the carriage porch,
in front of the eastern entrance door.

The house stands east and west; the east
front, with broad gravel space before the
principal door, looking on to the smooth lawn,
walks, shrubberies, and trees, which stretch
down as far as the road. On the north (the
side of the iron gates), on the west, and on
the east, kept ground lies round the house.

Beyond the west garden, and stretching

B

southwards, is the park. It is surrounded by
a wall, and within, or hard by, are some well-
built and pleasant houses, a parsonage, a
house for the Comptroller of the Household,
others for the suite and various officials.

A lake lately made near the centre of the
park is overhung with trees, and crowned by
a centre island. Another pretty lake adorns
the west garden, and varies the formal parterres and trim slopes with its bright waters.

One of the broad shrubbery walks on the
opposite side of the house winds between
rare pines and garden shrubs to the spacious
stables.

Beyond the boxes and stalls for sixty
horses, there is a dainty little stable lined with
pale-green and milk-white shining tiles; and
in stalls, ornamented with silver, are the four
tiny ponies which form the team of Her
Royal Highness the Princess of Wales.

These, and other small curiosities in the
shape of ponies, are hardly so large as the
St. Bernard, Thibet, and Newfoundland dogs,

who live in a long series of kennels not far
off. These rare dogs, from many countries,
fill the air with their eager barking; whilst
the two big black bears in a pit hard by, in-
different to spectators, calmly climb their ac-
customed pole.

Across the road on the east side of the
house, is the kitchen garden, with its excellent ranges of fruit-houses and glazed walls,
where strawberries ripen, peaches and necta-
rines blush, and vines, in all the perfection of
large leaves and fine and profuse fruit, cur-
tain the roofs of the vast graperies, a triumph
of training and bearing.

Rows of apple trees, trained in pyramids
to more than twenty feet in height, and re-
calling the aspect of those by the roadsides
of northern France, are planted across the
garden. These have broad strips of ground
for their exclusive use, the lower branches
fastened to an iron hoop near the ground,
while the upper ones, in succession, tied down
to one another, stoop to offer their fruit.

The fan-trained plum-trees, and the regular horizontal arrangement of the limbs of the pear-trees, ornament with neat and symmetrical effect a large space of the double walls which enclose the garden.

A few steps beyond, close to the spot from whence the Home Farm has so often sent out winners to the London and country agricultural shows, the Princess's dairy, newly built, furnishes a charming sight, the building including, besides its primary use, a sitting-room beautifully decorated with pictures and hand-painted tiles.

Many of the oaks which dot the garden and park are fine old trees, which have flourished there hundreds of years before the present house rose on a site previously occupied by more than one manor house.

That which existed in 1869—a building inadequate in size, and modernized into blankness as to any record of the past—was pulled down in that year, and replaced by the present hall, which holds precisely the same position and aspect. It is a good-looking, red brick house, with white stonework, windows of modern form, and a picturesque irregular outline. A suite of drawing-rooms faces the lake and parterres, and a broad corridor unites these rooms to the saloon or entrance hall. There is a beautiful coloured drawing by M. Zichy,* which gives a sketch of the saloon, with its royal inmates at afternoon tea. The design of this picture is original. At the top is a painting of Sandringham Hall; beneath it the Prince's escutcheon; and six vignettes, divided by bronze and green branches of foliage, represent the occupations and amusements of the day. The royal figures are unmistakeable likenesses; the soft, delicate colouring, and light free touch, suit the fanciful style of the composition.

Besides other rooms on the ground floor which contribute to the requisite completeness of the house, there are two libraries, which

* M. Michel Zichy, Court Painter to the late Emperor Alexander of Russia, and now living in Paris.

occupy the chief space between the saloon and the corner of the house next to the lime avenue. The cheerful east windows light up the interiors, which are models of comfort and good arrangement, and which contain a collection consisting mainly of the standard works of English and French literature, a good historical division, many presentation copies of modern books, and some valuable English county histories.

Two important additions, in 1883 and 1885, have carried on the never-ending work of improvement at the Hall and in the village;—this, a reading room and refreshment room at West Newton, forming an excellent agricultural club and entertainment hall;—that, a ballroom, much needed to complete the house, such an occasion as a ball having previously been celebrated in the entrance hall.

The County ball at Sandringham, which every succeeding November diffuses so much enjoyment and gratification, is now held in a room which forms a fitting framework to the bright picture. A new wing, at right angles with the east side of the house, contains a ballroom, 66 feet by 30 feet, the interior of which is so delicately coloured, so quaintly ornamented, so cheerfully lighted, as to seem like fairyland.

In this cool and stately hall, the recessed alcoves facing each other, are furnished, one with windows, the other with a massive fireplace. A large bay window at one end, filled with diapered glass, sheds an artificial light just above the long crimson seat from whence the Princess rises to dance, or to move with gracious kindness among her guests.

At the opposite end is placed the minstrels' gallery, from whence the flood of brilliant dance-music pours out, ever fresh and varied, as, it is said, the Prince's memory is tenacious and his taste fastidious, **with reference to those inspiring strains.**

CHAPTER III.

WEST NEWTON, SANDRINGHAM, AND ADJACENT CHURCHES.

URNING now from the house and its attractions, the adjacent villages and churches on the estate must be brought under notice. To arrive at the nearest of these a distant park gate must be reached, close to which, on a southern slope, clusters the village of West Newton.

The church stands high upon an eminence, and in its neighbourhood are the cottages of various plans—some grouped in a formal row of blocks of two, others, more recent, less regular in appearance—which, one and all, present an appearance of neatness and comfort, and whose design provides them with all requisite details for the convenience, due accommodation, and health of their occupants. Here it is that the Princess herself is often to be found, dispensing the personal attention and sympathy to her humbler neighbours, which have helped to make her worshipped around Sandringham; as an excellent judgment, good business qualities, and a mindfulness of individuals and their services, have secured for the Prince the respect and affection of his tenants and cottagers.

The church of West Newton contains a nave divided from the aisles by a handsome, rather low, fifteenth century arcade; it gains beauty from two windows, east and west, of stained glass, singularly pure and graceful in colour, and good in design; the latter given by the brothers and sisters of the Prince of Wales.

This church has been quite recently carefully restored, with new roofs, and seats of pitch pine. The colour and design of these, as also the unglazed tile flooring, combine happily with the simple beauty of the stone arches, and the unity of effect is none the less kept for being touched here and there with a choice bit of carved work, or other ornament.

Sandringham Church, dedicated to St. Mary Magdalen, is in the park, and is approached through the garden by an avenue of fine old Scotch firs. It stands nobly, on a rising ground, a late perpendicular church, with battlements round the walls and tower. It was first restored in 1855 "by Lady Harriet Cowper, wife of the Hon. Spencer Cowper, to commemorate their only child," but has been much beautified since it came into the hands of the Prince of Wales.

Some of the glass mosaic, in gold and colours, which the artists of Murano now produce to compete with their predecessors in that lovely and intricate Italian art, adorns the reredos. Munich glass, amber and brown, fills in with good effect the nave windows.

There are four small memorial windows in the chancel, above the seats of carved work which are occupied by their Royal Highnesses ; one of those on the south side, and a marble cross in the churchyard, are in remembrance of the infant prince whose brief earthly life terminated on April 7th, 1871.

A life-sized marble profile head, in bas-relief, occupies the north wall of the chancel, and recalls the beautiful memory of the Princess Alice of Hesse, and there is a brass lectern in the church which bears an interesting inscription, and marks almost the only shadow which has ever fallen across this royal threshold :—

To the glory of GOD,
A thank offering for his mercy,
14 December, 1871,
ALEXANDRA.

" When I was in trouble I called upon the Lord, and He heard me."

Some fine sepia and coloured drawings exist of Sandringham Church. They are much in the manner of Cotman, and were made in 1842, by the daughters of Mr. Dawson Turner, to illustrate the copy of Blomefield's " Norfolk," in which that well-known collector of Norfolk lore preserved the aspect of so many objects which have since gone to actual decay.

The third church of the group, Babingley, stands picturesquely, when seen from the road, between Sandringham and Castle Rising. The little edifice, with a steep-roofed ruined chancel, appears between the tall willows bordering the stream which runs parallel with the church at about two hundred yards' distance. On approaching nearer, it is evident that the sea, which came up to Castle Rising close by, flowed to the foot of the field on which stands the church. This is a sort of promontory with low ground on either side.

Tradition points this out as the spot where Felix, the French missionary, who first introduced Christianity into East Anglia, landed, and built a wooden church, and the character of the ground confirms the supposition.

Beda relates how Felix, the original mover of the flood of Christian light which has civilized Norfolk, came over to Canterbury from Burgundy in 631, to be ordained bishop by the successor of Augustine. He had made acquaintance in Burgundy with Sigeberht, King of East Anglia, and had converted him to Christianity.

Honorius sent Felix "to preach the word of life to the nation of the Angles," where "the pious husbandman of the spiritual field reaped therein a large harvest of believers, delivering all that province, according to the hidden signification of his name (Felix), from long iniquity and infelicity, and bringing it to the faith and works of righteousness, and the gifts of everlasting happiness."

This event, narrated by the learned monk and scholar less than a hundred years after its occurrence, receives the touches which fix it to actual spots, from later historians, who, in repeating the story of Beda, add the traditions yielded by the neighbourhood itself.

Sir Henry Spelman alludes to the tradition; Camden says in his "Britannia," published in 1607 (the Norfolk section of which owes something to the collections of Spelman) : —"The first [Christian church] Felix is said to have built at Babingley, where he landed," and "at Babingley, Felix, the Apostle of the East Angles, coming about the year 630, converted the inhabitants to Christianity; and, as hath been said, built there the first Christian church in those parts, of which succeeding ages made St. Felix the patron."

Blomefield, in describing Shernborne, a village in Norfolk, asserts that "Spelman and the rest of our historians relate that a church was built here, the second that was erected in the kingdom of the East Angles, the first being a little before founded by the encouragement of the said bishop at Babingley, where he first landed."

In Peter Le Neve's handwriting, in his "Collections for Norfolk," is the following entry, — "Babingley. This was the first

church built in these parts by Felix, the
Burgundian, as saith the manuscript belonging
to the family of Shernburn."

The hills in the neighbourhood have long
been called "the Christian hills," a name
which has been handed down from century to
century, in memory (according to Sir Henry
Spelman, who described them in his "Icenia")
of the first crusade in Norfolk.

The present church stands in the lonely
field, unapproached even by a gravel path or
made road of any kind; it contains no remains of great antiquity, but a stone coffin,
which is perfect excepting the lid, and which
stood some years ago in the churchyard.

The eastern window and chancel, the nave,
arches, and aisle chapels must originally have
been handsome; the chancel arch was bricked
up, and an ugly square-headed window in-
serted at some long-past period, when the
building was altered and patched in the poorest possible style.

It seems to bear witness that a church was

not really wanted there, so close to the others, and all the populations being small—and also to the fact that in the reign of Elizabeth the fabrics were offensive to the Catholic families, through whose influence so many of them are in ruins, and who resented the attendance enforced.

In truth, a church in this position seems scarcely more needed now than it has been in past centuries; and a fine stone cross to mark the interesting site of Felix's wooden church would be as appropriate a memorial of the first planting of Christianity in Norfolk, as a building which has nothing whatever to do with the original structure.

At Wolferton, which lies in a picturesque and agreeable situation about two miles from Sandringham, and where the railway bringing travellers from London, has its station,—there is a finer and more interesting church than any of the preceding. It is, in the main, in late decorated style, fourteenth century, and stands on an abrupt eminence. After a fire in 1486 (mentioned by Blomefield, and lately verified by an entry in the Instituting Book), the parishioners had license from the Bishop "to collect the alms of good people for the rebuilding of their parish church, lately burnt down by a sudden fire."

Parts of the church were therefore rebuilt late in the 15th century. There was a specially fine nave roof, one of the finest in Norfolk, but this was lamentably spoilt in Mr. Motteux's time, who, by way of "restoring" the church, sold the lead, cut off all the rich ornament from the grand beams (leaving, however, the supporting statues), and fitted up the church with the poorest deal seats.

The screens are noticeable; that at the end of the south aisle is flowing in design, but its mouldings give it a date subsequent to the fire. In Norfolk, woodwork retained its earlier form very late. There is a similar instance in St. Nicholas Church at Lynn, where a screen exists which would in form, not in moulding, be a century earlier than its true date.   c

The east window of St. Peter's, Wolferton, although modern, is an accurate copy, in all the details of its masonry, which are beautiful and very uncommon, of the original window. This was done by the late rector, Mr. Dickinson, who had the remains taken out, careful drawings made, and the design exactly reproduced.* The Prince of Wales has replaced the deal benches of Mr. Motteux with oak seats ; has caused the roof to be repaired and strengthened as to its construction, placing also new roofs to the chancel and aisles ; and, besides other additions, has presented a stone pulpit and an organ, to complete the requisite furniture of the church.

* These particulars have been kindly communicated by Mr. E. M. Beloe, of King's Lynn.

CHAPTER IV.

IN days gone by, Sandringham has passed through the hands of many successive proprietors, some of whom can claim a link with English history. Not to go further back, the principal families connected with these manors from the fourteenth century to the nineteenth, were those of Clifton, Scales, Cobbe, and Hoste; and, in this century, up to 1861, Hoste, Henley, Motteux, and Cowper.

"Westhall Manor," including soil which had belonged to lords of the names of Tateshall and Butler, lying in, and forming part of, the three villages of Babingley, Wolferton, and Sandringham, was directed by Sir John Clifton, in his will, dated August 16, 1447, and proved in the September following, to be sold, and it appears that these lands, and the advowson of Babingley were bought by Thomas, Lord Scales, who presented to the living in 1459. This manor was held successively by Lord Scales, his daughter Elizabeth, her husband Earl Rivers (who survived her, and took the name of Scales), and by distant heirs, until the family occupation ceased after the lapse of a hundred years, when the property was acquired by the Cobbes.

Middleton Tower, in Norfolk, was the Scales' family seat; a fine building standing in the level fields not far from King's Lynn. The six escallop shells, the picturesque coat of arms of the Lord Scales, are still to be seen over the gateway; the warm colouring of the noble old tower is reflected in the moat beneath; the projecting oriel windows have been well preserved, and the modern additions, solid and simple, have been achieved without drawback to the beauty of the ancient edifice.

Probably it was at Middleton that Elizabeth Scales, destined to be the heiress of divers estates in Norfolk and elsewhere, and the latest of her name to succeed to them, saw the light. There is evidence in the Lynn records that her father, Lord Scales, occupied a dwelling-house there in 1445, and a tradition has been handed down in the neighbourhood that "Middleton Tower" was rebuilt by him with the materials of the "most royal and beautiful" manor house at Roydon, near Castle Rising, when that mansion, a possession of the Wodehouses, was pulled down by his advice and with his assistance in 1454.

. Elizabeth, the last of her family, led a life, whose years, as they passed over her, caught the red reflection of the events of her time. She lived in the very thick of the Wars of the Roses, and her short career, marked at frequent stages by the occurrence

of a furious battle or a merciless execution
in which her nearest friends suffered, was
only softened by the atmosphere of intellec-
tual light thrown around her by her scholarly
husband, and by the kindness she received
at the court of Queen Elizabeth Woodville.
The only companion of her childhood, her
brother, died young; her father was murdered in 1460; the death of her first husband,
Henry Bourchier, followed; her father-in-law,
Earl Rivers, and her brother-in-law, John
Woodville, were executed in 1469. Had she
lived a few years longer, she would have seen
her husband brought to the block at Pontefract, and his two royal nephews put to death
in the Tower.

But there were some merry days at Middleton before these tragedies were enacted.
The family had emerged from local obscurity
at the end of Henry the Fifth's reign, when
Thomas, Lord Scales, the father of Elizabeth,
served in the war going on in France. He
was subsequently Seneschal of Normandy,

and throughout his life adhered to the house of Lancaster, losing it eventually in serving that cause.

One winter, when he was about forty-six years old, in a quiet interval soon after Henry the Sixth's marriage to Margeret of Anjou, Lord Scales and his wife were living at Middleton. In a south-east direction lay the higher ground where rose the Blackborough Priory of nuns, founded by a previous Lady Scales; west of them, at three miles' distance, bristling with the architecture of the middle ages in all its bloom and beauty, before religious disunion had defaced it; prosperous in its self-government—stood the town of Lynn.

The mayor and council had organized a play to be acted on Christmas Day, 1445, before the Lord Scales at Middleton, representing scenes from the Nativity of our Lord. Large sums were paid, by order of the mayor, for the requisite dresses, ornaments, and scenery, some of which were supplied by the " Nathan " of Lynn, and others prepared

and brought expressly. "John Clerk" per-
formed the angel Gabriel, and a lady of the
name of Gilbert the Virgin Mary. Their
parts were to be sung. Four other performers
were also paid for ther services, and the whole
party, headed by the mayor, set off, with their
paraphernalia, in a cart, harnessed to four
or more horses, for Middleton on Christmas
morning. The breakfast of the carters was
paid for at the inn by the town, but the
magnates from Lynn and the actors were
entertained at the castle.*

It was in the courtyard that this quaint
representation took place; the musical dia-
logues, the songs and hymns, the profusion of
ornaments, personal and otherwise, recorded
as pressed on to the stage, the grotesque
angel and virgin, must have furnished a lively
hour under the castle walls on that long-ago
Christmas day.

In contrast with such *fêtes* were the occupations of the last years of Lord Scales' life. He arranged for his little daughter one of those children's marriages usual in those days, and in the summer of 1460, he was engaged in defending the Tower of London, on the part of the king, against Lord War-wick, and Edward, Earl of March, the future successor of Henry.

But on the surrender of the Tower, and the bringing thither the captive king some days later, Lord Scales slipped away privately by water, and, at the moment of his escape, was identified, and murdered in a boat in the dark by the watermen of Lord Warwick. He was buried in an adjoining church, instead of in the stately priory of Blackborough, which had enshrined so many of his predecessors.

The second husband of Elizabeth Scales, Anthony Woodville, was the son of Richard Woodville, first Earl Rivers, King Edward the Fourth's treasurer and constable, and the father of his queen, Elizabeth. The Wood-villes were a Kentish family, of gentle blood

but poor circumstances, who were raised by
the marriage of Richard to the widowed
Duchess of Bedford, Princess Jaquetta, of
Luxembourg. Anthony, their eldest son,
married the Lady Scales in 1462, two years
before his family was honoured by the king's
selection of one of the beautiful daughters of
the house, as his wife.

Anthony Woodville, Lord Rivers and
Scales, was a person of marked distinction in
very various departments of life. A noble
quality pervaded the texture of his character
and shone in his actions. Of "constant
feythe" in his loyalty; prominent in his brav-
ery and skill in the battlefield and at the
tournament; conspicuous, as were all the
Woodvilles, for good looks; a linguist and
author, a warm friend to the progress of
learning, he contributed to give the impulse
in England to that love of letters which was
struggling into life even against the adverse
tide of civil war, of which Caxton's industry
was at once the sign and the promoter, and

which the coming epoch of peace under the
Tudors was to sun into blossom and luxuriance. Shortly after his marriage, he assumed
the title of Lord Scales. By this he was
called for seven years, signing thus the presentation of John Pyncote to the living of
Babingley in 1467, until in 1469, he became
Earl Rivers, "gentle Rivers," his sister the
queen calls him; "Rivieres," he calls himself;
retaining Scales as a second title, and quart-
ering on his shield the scarlet field and silver
shells.

It was in the autumn of 1470 that he
accompanied Edward the Fourth to Lynn.
Edward had retreated before Lord Warwick
in Lincolnshire, and was on his way to seek
a shelter beyond the sea. Lord Rivers, no
doubt well acquainted with the locality, showed
the king and three thousand men the way
into Lynn late in the evening of Sunday, the
30th of September. They remained in Lynn
until Tuesday morning, when, at eight o'clock,
the king and some few attendants, including

Lord Rivers, left the monastery where they
had been lodged, and went down to the
staith, whence they went on board some ships
in the port, and put to sea.

On the Monday a meeting had been held
at the Guildhall, when arrangements were
made for strengthening the watches round the
walls, which were to guard the town and its
royal inmate from a surprise that night.

The king was received, on landing on the
Dutch coast, by Louis of Bruges, Seigneur
de la Gruthuyse, who conducted him first to
the Hague, then to his country house near
Bruges, and afterwards to the Hotel Grut-
huyse, in the town. There Edward and his
companions remained the honoured guests of
Louis, who was the governor of the town of
Bruges, and Governor of Holland under the
Duke of Burgundy.

It was during this sojourn in the Low
Countries that Lord Rivers made the acquaintance of Caxton, which led to their
friendship, and to the eventual publication by

the latter of the two volumes which attest the earl's literary capacity.

. There is something which excites attention and reflection in the contrasts which those times displayed, contrasts of which the character and fate of Lord Rivers afford a notable example. That the most ingenious and beneficent invention the world has ever seen, developed by acute thought, by silent industry, in secluded withdrawal from the crowd, should have worked its way into light simultaneously with the constant practice of coarse butchery, the rude injustice, the savage contempt for human life and the preciousness of human qualities, which prevailed, in England especially, is as surprising as was the store of honey discovered in the bleeding carcase of the lion, or the star which hung, radiant and auspicious, above the holocaust of the Innocents.

Caxton had lived many years in Bruges, known to the King of England as what we should now call " English Consul " at Bruges, and as ambassador thither to Philip of Burgundy in certain commercial negotiations; and known later to the king's sister Margaret, Duchess of Burgundy, as a man of letters.

This was Lord Rivers' second visit; he had gone there when Lord Scales, soon after the death of Philip the Good, Duke of Burgundy, to joust at the tournament on the marriage of Margaret, festivities which are described with much spirit by John Paston, in one of the Paston Letters.

Bruges, beautiful now, was then in its palmiest days. The busy city was alive with commercial enterprise and movement; the circular harbour and the canals were crowded with trading vessels, the broad streets were flanked by substantial and richly decorated houses. The tall belfry, a marvel of elegance and strength, rang out its piercing tunes 300 feet above the heads of the merchants in the exchange at its base. The figures in front of the town hall in the same grand square glittered fresh from the hand of the sculptor;

in monastery studios and quiet workshops the products of the easel and the printing press were stealing into glorious existence.

Colard Mansion was on the eve of begining to print his magnificent folios in the little room over the porch of St. Donatus' Church, while a group of workers, so numerous as to form a guild, contributed, as authors, scribes, illuminators, painters of vignettes, binders, and engravers, to the production of books.

Among the handsome houses none was handsomer than the Hotel Gruthuyse. There the king was adequately lodged, and there a trio of friends—the host, Lord Rivers, and Caxton — gratified their taste for literature among the manuscripts which had been collected by the Seigneur de la Gruthuyse, This latter was scarcely less powerful as a patron of literature than Philip the Good himself. He had employed the artists of Bruges and Ghent to furnish his library with the volumes, inscribed on the finest vellum, enriched with choice illuminations, and enclosed in costly bindings, which are now to be found in the manuscript department of the Bibliothèque Nationale de Paris.*

When Edward the Fourth returned to England, and was again established on the throne, he invited Gruthuyse to Windsor.

Preserved in the British Museum is a manuscript, written by a herald who was present, giving a vivid account of Gruthuyse's entertainment there, in the month of September, 1473. The narrative brings again on to the scene Lady Rivers and Scales, who was present at these gaieties.

" The Quene ordeined a greate Bankette in her owne chamber, at the which Bankette were the Kinge, the Quene, my Lady Elizabeth, the King's eldest daughter, the Duchess

---

* Nearly the whole of this library passed into the hands of Louis XII., and about a hundred volumes are in the Bibliothèque Nationale. The history of them has been written by M. Léopold Delisle, the present Administrateur Général of the Library, in a book entitled "Le Cabinet de Manuscrits de la Bibliothèque Nationale." 3 vols. Quarto.

of Exeter, the Lady Rivers, the Lord Grauthuse, settinge at one messe . . . there was a syde-table, at the which sette a greate vue of ladies, all on the one syde." After the banquet, they amused themselves with games and dancing.

This is the last recorded notice of Elizabeth Scales; she died within a year of the banquet. Her marriage, which had lasted nearly twelve years, was a childless one, and she left her husband in possession of her Norfolk manors. He was thus the third of her name, and certainly the most distinguished, who possessed the manor at Sandringham.

CHAPTER V.

EARL RIVERS.

FTER the death of his wife, Lord Rivers started immediately on a pilgrimage to the shrine of St. James, at Compostella in Spain, and, on the voyage, lighted upon better consolation than even the saint was likely to afford him. Lord Macaulay has said that his love of literature preserved him from sinking under bereavement, and quotes the passage from Hesiod which expresses that "if to one whose grief is fresh, as he sits silent with sorrow-stricken heart, the henchman of the muses celebrates the men of old and the gods who

possess Olympus; straightway he forgets his
melancholy, and remembers not all his grief,
beguiled by the blessed gift of the goddesses
of song."

Lord Rivers experienced this truth, for
whilst at sea, a book was lent him by a fellow-
passenger, which took his fancy. It was a
selection and translation from various Greek
authors into French; and its further translation by himself into English, as well as other
translations from the French, occupied him
thenceforth in somewhat arduous and lengthy
literary work.

The arrival of Caxton from Bruges in 1476,
freighted with material unpretending enough
to look at, but containing within it the seed
of an illimitable influence, stimulated these
labours, whose results were to be immortal-
ized by the introduction of the new art into
England.

There are two manuscripts of much interest,
both connected with Lord Rivers, in the
libraries of London. The one is a manu-

script of his first book, " The Dictes and
Sayings of the Philosophers," with a portrait
of himself, and is deposited in the archiepis-
copal library at Lambeth; the other, the
French manuscript from which he translated
his second book, " The Proverbs of Christine
of Pisa," is to be found among the treasures
of the British Museum.

The first-mentioned work was written out,
on small vellum folio sheets, by a scribe named
Haywarde, whose name is appended to it,
with the date of the completion of the tran-
scription, December 20th, 1477. Four weeks
earlier the same book had astonished the
world by its appearance in print. The delicate painting in the folio, illuminated in gold
and colours, depicts Lord Rivers presenting
his printed book to Edward the Fourth. He
kneels at the king's feet, in a coat emblazoned
with his well-known quarterings, in armour
and blue leggings or stockings, the dark hair
cut straight and low across the forehead (a
fashion followed by men in those days) in

his hand a ponderous volume which the king takes from him.* On the left side of the king stands the little Prince Edward, seven years old, in a scarlet mantle and gold coronet, and, kneeling by Lord Rivers, a figure in a black robe edged with fur, possibly Caxton.† This book was printed by Caxton soon after his arrival in England, and is the first dated book printed by him. A copy of the first edition, that belonging to Lord Spencer, at Althorp, gives the month and day—November 18th. In the first edition the epilogue is as follows :—

" Here endeth the book named the dictes or sayengis of the philosophers emprynted by

---

* A facsimile of this book has been recently printed by Mr. Elliot Stock.

† This is a matter of dispute, as the head is bald, and it has been supposed to be the portrait of an ecclesiastic. The hair, however, is not cut formally, as in the case of a priest, and the fur trimming to the gown is a very unorthodox vestment. This vignette was engraved for Strutt's " Regal and Ecclesiastical Antiquities of England," and is described by Horace Walpole. Both these authors consider the kneeling figure to be Caxton.

me William Caxton at Westmiestre the yere of our lorde 1477, whiche book is late translated out of frensh into englyssh by the noble and puissant lord Lord Antone Erle of Ryvers lord of Scales."

The manuscript in the British Museum is presumably the actual one from which Lord Rivers made his translation. The book is a collection of " Proverbes Morales," written in French by Christine of Pisa, an authoress born in Italy, but whose life was spent in France during the end of the fourteenth and first years of the fifteenth centuries. She composed " Enseignemens Moraux" for the benefit of her son, political treatises, and heroic poems to celebrate the victories of Joan of Arc.

The volume (to be found among the Harleian MSS.), a splendid specimen, contains the autograph of Earl Rivers :—

M

NVLLE LA VAV*l*T

ÆRIVIERES

and on the right of his signature, that of his mother, Jacquetta, Duchess of Bedford.

The book was considered by Sir Frederick Madden to have belonged to Isabella, queen of Charles the Sixth of France. When she yielded the French crown to Henry the Sixth, the Duke of Bedford went to Paris as Regent, and had possession of the royal library there, from which he abstracted, or was given, the volume in question, which he presented to his wife, who left it to her son Anthony.

Lord Rivers' translation of this book, which is in metre, was also dated by Caxton :—

" At Westmestre, of feverer the xx daye, and of Kyng Edward the xvii yere. Emprinted by Caxton in feverer the colde season."*

The circumstances which led to the writing of these books are thus made clear. Anthony Woodville's possession of the choice volume

---

* That is, Feb. 1477-8. Blades says the only copies known are in the libraries of Earl Spencer, the Earl of Jersey, and Mr. Christie Miller.

containing the lucubrations of Christine of Pisa ; and his desire to give to others, at a time when the classics of Rome and Greece were scarcely attainable in England, some of the wisdom of the ancients.

Among those whom he hoped to benefit by these labours was his royal nephew, Edward, Prince of Wales, to whom he had been appointed "governor." As the boy grew older, Lord Rivers remained for some time with him at Ludlow Castle, in Shropshire, where the young prince pursued his studies under the enlightened direction of his uncle, while propitiating the Welsh by his close proximity to his principality. With them was also Prince Edward's chamberlain, Sir Richard Vaughan, who had been in his service from infancy, carrying him in his arms at Windsor, where the boy, too young to walk, was brought out on special occasions.*

* "My lord prince also, borne by his chamberlayn, Master Vaghan, Sept. 1472." MS. "Of the coming into

When King Edward the Fourth died, the little household from the borders of Wales was summoned to London, and on their way halted to sleep at Stony Stratford, in Buckinghamshire. It was in the month of April, 1483, that the prince, thirteen years old, his friends, servants, and a band of horsemen, rode slowly southwards through the midland counties towards London.

In the fresh spring weather the country was wakening into leaf and beauty— emblem of hope and life ; but too truly was the destiny of the young prince shadowed out by the uncertain season :—

> " What is this passing scene?
> A peevish April day !
> A little sun—a little rain,
> And then night sweeps along the plain,
> And all things fade away.
> Man (soon discussed)
> Yields up his trust,
> And all his hopes and fears lie with him in the dust."

England of the Lord Graythuyse." In the British Museum. Add. 6113, f. 103b.

As the prince arrived at Stony Stratford, Richard, Duke of Gloucester, his hunchbacked uncle, rode into Northampton, ten miles off, on his way from Scotland. Six hundred knights, all clad in deep mourning, formed Richard's ominous escort. Rivers rode over to Northampton to welcome him in the name of the little king, was entertained at supper, and returned the next morning, accompanied by his host.

Richard did homage to the king, but proceeded without delay to deprive the child, who burst into tears of distress, of his familiar and beloved attendants, placing Rivers and the faithful Vaughan under a strong guard, and despatching them towards Pontefract. Richard took the little prince to London; first, to show him, arrayed in his regal blue velvet cloak, to his subjects, and then to consign him to the sombre walls of the Tower.

Pontefract Castle was the eventual destination of Rivers, but he was first confined for two months in the Castle of Sheriff Hutton.

This place belonged to Richard of Gloucester, a strong castle eleven miles north of York, standing on the top of an eminence, its massive corner towers each containing a dungeon beneath the rooms; its windows, pierced through walls ten feet thick, looking from their height on to the distant forest of Galtrees to the west, then a tract of wood, moor, and bog, spreading for many miles into the North Riding.

There he remained, "somewhat musing and more mourning," to use his own expression, during the month of May and part of June. The records that we have of him this time being his will, and a sonnet containing a last expression of woe, courage, and resignation, transcribed from his own handwriting by a contemporary historian.*

In his will, dated at Sheriff Hutton, June 23rd, 1483, he bequeaths "the lands that were my first wife's, the Lady Scales, and

* Ross's "History," 8vo, 2nd ed., p. 213. The sonnet is given in Percy's "Reliques."

Thomas, Lord Scales', her brother, to my brother, Sir Edward Woodville;" but his manor of Wolverton and the advowson to be sold, to make an hospital at Rochester for thirteen poor folk.

It appears that the will was not proved and was set aside, as, although his brother was living in 1490, the estates of Lady Scales were inherited by two of her relations, Lady Oxford and Sir William Tyndal, on the accession of Henry VII., two years after the death of Earl Rivers.

In the first part of the will he directs that his body shall be buried at Westminster; but at the end of the will a change in the directions given darkly intimates that he had not only heard of the execution at Pontefract of his relative Lord Richard Grey, but had received the terrible notice that a similar ordeal was in store for himself: "My will is now to be buried before an image of our blessed Lady Mary with my Lord Richard in Pomfret, and Jesu have mercy on my soule!"

It was almost immediately after the date of his will that Lord Rivers was taken to Pontefract, where Richard of Gloucester's bloody sentence was inflicted upon him without reason, trial, or delay.

But Richard had not done with Rivers. It is a summer night on a Leicestershire moor. Bosworth town looks down from an adjacent eminence on an array of tents sprinkling the rough ground, and just visible in the darkness. The stillness of midnight settles down at last over the plain, over the hive of soldiers, over the faint gleam of the white tents, over the hideous figure and malignant countenance of the king, resting uneasily on the verge of the fatal day.

The defection of many of his adherents had already warned Richard of his danger; he knew the coming risk of desertion at the moment of battle; he knew the chances of war. In the dead of the night, under the possibility of impending death, conscience awoke, and showed him, one after another,

he crimes he had committed; or, as Shak-
speare in poetic allegory puts it, the souls
appeared of those whom he had sent to their
account.   Each ghost in turn rises before the
ent, speaks, and disappears—

"*The Ghost of Rivers rises.*—

  'Let me sit heavy on thy soul to-morrow,
  Rivers, that died at Pomfret!
  Despair, and die!'"

CHAPTER VI.

SANDRINGHAM IN THE SIXTEENTH CENTURY.

AS Rivers and his times fade from the scene, the last heirs of Elizabeth Scales, Lady Oxford, and Sir William Tyndal, gradually loosened their hold on the various Norfolk manors, until, in 1517, they finally parted with them at Sandringham, Babingley, and Wolferton to the Cobbe family, who had for some time possession of other lands lying in the same parishes.*

---

* As early as 1493 lands in Sandringham, Babingley, Wolferton, Newton, Appleton, and Anmer belonged to William Cobbe. The will of William Cobbe was proved

The owners of Sandringham have at various times formed alliances with many of the principal Norfolk families; the Cobbes, who were among the leading gentry of the county, intermarried with the Spelmans, Walpoles, Bedingfelds, and Astleys; in later days, Elizabeth, daughter of Sir Edward Walpole, of Houghton, and Susan, daughter of Anthony Hamond, married into the Hoste family, who had succeeded the Cobbes in the estate and manor house.

These several alliances led to relationships needless and hopeless to unravel, but some of them stand out clearly, and the connexion of the Cobbes with other Catholic families, either by relationship or on the ground of common political and religious opinion, can be traced.

There stands, not far from Swaffham, one of the earliest and finest of the old houses

---

(P.C.C.) 6th Nov., 1493. A pedigree, which belonged to the late Mr. Thomas Cobbe of Easton Lys, begins with William Cobbe of Sandringham, 1323.

of Norfolk, begun in Edward IV.'s reign* by one of a family whose fortunes, character, and doings have invested Oxburgh with an historical importance, as well as with the domestic interest which clings to walls within which generation after generation has lived and died.

A hundred years after this stately house was built, an unusually rapid series of deaths occurred in the Bedingfeld family; Sir Henry Bedingfeld, the "jaylor" of Queen Elizabeth, died in 1583; his son Edmund † in 1585; and the son and heir of the latter, Thomas, in April, 1590.

Thomas Bedingfeld had, among other sisters, Nazareth, who married Edward Yelverton, and Mary, who married Sir William Cobbe, of Sandringham.

Sir William Cobbe, Knight, was the son

---

* Edward IVth gave the licence to prepare materials for building in July, 1482.

† Of Ereswell, in Suffolk, one of the Bedingfield manors.

E

of Geoffrey Cobbe, who died in 1581. Geoffrey left all his manors to his son William, who was then a minor, and numerous legacies to others. To his sister Alice "one cup of silver gilt, with a cover, which I bought at Lynn Mart, weighing between fifteen and sixteen ounces."

The glories of Lynn Mart have departed since the days when the fairs held in the country towns gave opportunities of meeting to the gentry around, and provided them with goods not usually obtainable. Geoffrey Cobbe, if he could ride to Lynn now, as he did then, would not even find the porcelain which was sold there forty years ago, much less gold plate; although perhaps John Butler, the mountebank, who commended Norfolk for the "plenty of money stirring among the common people" in 1663, and the man who showed the dromedary "in most parts of England" at about the same time, have their counterparts in the shows which struggle feebly to Lynn every Valentine's Day.

The name of Mary Cobbe, Edmund Bedingfeld's daughter, is to be found in 1595
in the "Popish Recusant" Rolls,* those
yearly lists dating from the beginning of
Elizabeth's reign, of the Catholics who refused
to attend the worship of the Established
Church, who denied the spiritual supremacy
of the crown, and who were, in consequence,
subjected to cruel penalties.

The sympathies of both husband and wife
were with the Roman Catholics, although the
former was not an avowed Romanist; some
of their neighbours were friends whose watchword was their own, and who were, like them,
in danger of the impoverishing fine, or the
embargo on their movements; such were the
Walpoles at Anmer, the Yelvertons at Grimstone, the Pastons at Appleton. These, with
the Spelmans at Congham, and, a little further

---

* Many of these Norfolk rolls may be found printed
in Tymm's "East Anglian." A Norfolk and Suffolk list,
given at p. 176 of vol. ii., has the following:—"Sandringham. Mary Cobbes, the Wyffe of Willia' Cobbes,
esquier."

off, the le Stranges at Hunstanton, furnished society even in that wild and open part of Norfolk, distant from any town, during the time that William Cobbe lived as owner of Sandringham, from 1581 to 1607.

But to those who were in the secret of the movements and hopes of the Roman Catholic party in Norfolk, it was a society with an undertone of misgiving.

Anmer was, as has been mentioned, then occasionally the resort of those sons of the house who were perilling their lives as Jesuit priests, and its household lived in perpetual apprehension on their account.

The houses of "the ancient gentlemen's families in Norfolk," who clung to the old faith, were continually liable to be searched for suspected characters. Three or four miles from Sandringham, at Grimstone, lived Lady Cobbe's sister, Nazareth Yelverton, the "virtuous and loving wife" of Edward Yelverton, described, as well as her sister, as a "recusant."

Edward Yelverton, whose name is in the

list of "Popish recusants in Norfolk and
Suffolk, 1596, was the son of William Yelverton of Rougham, and a noticeable member of
the family, which was then very influential in
Norfolk.* He was born at Rougham,† and
moved from thence to Grimstone, then to
Appleton, unconsciously approaching nearer
and nearer to his grave, which lies beneath
the pavement of Sandringham Church. There,
after a faithful and life-long devotion to the
Catholic cause, its interests, its rites, and its
champions, which had cost him an imprison-
ment and many other sacrifices, he rested in
peace at last.

In the same year that old Christopher
Walpole died of a broken heart at Anmer,‡

---

* They were not all Roman Catholics, as Launcelot,
Edward Yelverton's brother was rector of Sculthorpe,
Norfolk.

† An entry in Le Neve's "Norfolk Collections" mentions that Edward Yelverton the "Recusant" lived at
Grimstone and Appleton. He also had a "small howse"
at Wolferton.

‡ "One Generation of a Norfolk House," p. 261.

after the trial and execution of his son Henry at York, which had painfully impressed the little community round Sandringham, the Cobbes were watching the building of a fine new house at Appleton, not two miles distant, by Sir Edward Paston. This house far exceeded that at Sandringham in size and beauty —"a very agreeable handsome pile," * "a very fair mansion." † Sir Edward acquired the land from his uncle Clement Paston, of Caistor and Oxnead, a well-known naval commander, in the reigns of Mary and Elizabeth.

Although it appears that the Pastons of Oxnead were Protestants in the later years of Queen Elizabeth, ‡ there is some colour for

---

* Blomefield's " Norfolk."

† Sir Henry Spelman's " History of Sacrilege."
"Progredienti versus Boream, Appleton, ubi splendidus ædes." From Peter Le Neve's " Manuscript Collections."

‡ Sir William Paston of Oxnead presented to the living of Oxnead in 1609, and had a licence in the nineteenth of Elizabeth to purchase the advowson of Paston from Thomas Woodhouse.

believing that the Pastons of Appleton and
Barningham were, in fact, if not in profession,
Romanists.

The grand-daughter of Sir Edward Paston
of Appleton, married, about the year 1634,
Sir Henry Bedingfeld, the first baronet,* a
noted Catholic, and two of their daughters
were nuns; Sir Edward Paston never presented to the living of Appleton; the branch
of the family at Barningham (the descendants
of Sir Edward Paston's eldest son Thomas)
were included in a printed list drawn up in
1715 of "Roman Catholics, non-jurors, and
others" who refused to take the oaths to
George I. †

The Pastons liked building beautiful houses.
Clement had, at the time of the building of
the Appleton house, just finished the magnificent family seat at Oxnead.

* Tombstone in Oxburgh Church.

† This list includes Jane Paston, of Town Barningham,
widow, with an income of 322*l.*; Edward, of Barningham, with an income of 1413*l.* 13*s.* 7¼*d.*; Clement, of
Barningham, with an income of 100*l.* See Pedigree in
Appendix.

Sir Edward Paston is said to have built Barningham Hall, in the east of Norfolk in 1612; and also Thorpe Hall, near Norwich.

The selection of Appleton as a mansion-house is accounted for as follows: he had commenced building a house at Binham, on the Priory ground which Henry VIII. had granted to his father, when an accident occurred which so shocked him that he relinquished the intention. While clearing some of the ground, a piece of wall fell upon a workman and killed him. Edward Paston's conscience smote him; he would have no more to do with secularizing consecrated ground. He therefore built his house at Appleton* a few months before his uncle's

---

* The date on the gatehouse was 1596; Clement Paston died in 1597. The house was destroyed by fire in 1707, when the family removed to Horton, in Wiltshire. The catastrophe is described by Le Neve. "1726. Appleton Hall burnt down to the ground on . . . . . day of . . . . . 1707. The family had all like to have burnt in their beds if a shepherd had not waked them."

death, and lived there until he was past eighty, close to the gates of the Cobbes.

With the le Stranges of Hunstanton Hall the Cobbes of Sandringham had been on neighbourly terms for more than a century.

In 1520 Mr. and Mrs. Cobbe (Mr. Cobbys and his wyff) stayed at Hunstanton, where they met the Prior of Coxford and Sir Henry Sharnbourn, and had for dinner a crane, six plover, and a brace of rabbits.* Mr. Cobbe made some profit out of his sheep-farm at Dersingham, for he supplied about this time twenty wethers for the hospitable table at Hunstanton, for which he also sent occasionally a present of a piece of porpoise, a fish which at that time was frequently served at the choicest dinners, dressed with bread crumbs and vinegar.

---

* There were living at Sandringham then an old couple, Mr. and Mrs. Jeffrie Cobbe, and their son William, who married Sir John Spelman's daughter. The visitors were accompanied to Hunstanton by Mr. Robert Brampton, who married Jeffrie Cobbe's daughter. Jeffrie Cobbe died in 1538, his son William in 1546.

In 1533 "Mestrys Cobe, and hyr syster, with others of the countreye," were guests at Hunstanton, and it was probably there that the Cobbes made the acquaintance of the Bedingfeld family, many of whom, especially "Edmund Bedingfeld," were constantly staying there.*

In the time of Sir William and Lady Cobbe, Hunstanton changed its masters quickly. Young Thomas le Strange, who married Edward Yelverton's sister, died in 1582; his brother, Sir Nicholas, ten years later, when Hamon, a boy of nine years old, became the owner of the venerable hall, with its gateway, its priest's room, and chapel hung with crimson velvet, its fine oak staircase and long panelled withdrawing room, where the beautifully executed family pedigree gradually grew beneath the cornice.

Sir Hamon le Strange was the ward of Sir Henry Spelman (then Mr. Spelman), of celebrated memory, and the Spelmans of

---

* Hunstanton account books and privy purse accounts.

Congham were also near neighbours and near relations of Sir William Cobbe.

The antiquary, born in 1564, was the son of Mr. Henry Spelman of Congham, and first cousin of Sir William Cobbe's father. Sir Henry Spelman spent thirty years in Norfolk, from 1582 to 1612, partly at Congham and partly at Hunstanton Hall. This learned knight, with his square beard, ruff, and skull-cap turned up with lace, was a well-known figure in his native county, where he gleaned, and preserved in his publications, many interesting local particulars which would otherwise have been lost, using these facts to point a moral in favour of the opinions which he held.

CHAPTER VII.

COLONEL COBBE.

SIR WILLIAM COBBE, Knight, could not have been more than forty years old when he died, in 1607, as attested by the register at Sandringham. Another William Cobbe, his grandson, has a less shadowy personality, and although no continuous narrative can be given of his life, he is known as one of those active and devoted soldiers who crowd the canvas where the two great figures —emblems severally of rugged strength, will, and intellect; of kingly fortitude and sorrow —rise with such terrible emphasis in the foreground.

The period of the last seven years of Charles I.'s reign was to the Cobbes and Bedingfelds, as to other active partisans of the king, fraught with adventure and suffering. A second alliance had then taken place between these families ; Colonel William Cobbe, who was born in 1613, and lived to 1665, married Elizabeth Bedingfeld, the daughter of Sir Henry Bedingfeld, Knight, of Oxburgh.

Two branches of the Cobbes were prominent in the seventeenth century on the royalist side ; those settled in Yorkshire and in Norfolk.

In Yorkshire, Sir Francis Cobbe, nearly related to Colonel Cobbe, of Sandringham, was Governor of York in 1644 ; his son, or grandson, an ensign in the king's army in 1640, and another of the family, Isaac Cobbe, was a lieutenant at the same time.* Sir

---

* "Army Lists of the Roundheads and Cavaliers, containing the names of the Officers in the Royal and Parliamentary Armies." Edited by Edward Peacock, F.S.A., 1874.

William Cobbe, of Adderbury, in Oxford-
shire, was a Roundhead, but his son Thomas
was created a baronet by Charles II.   He,
and the Yorkshire Cobbes, gained in position
and circumstances by their attitude towards
the Stuarts.   Colonel Cobbe, of Sandringham, on the contrary, lost much by it ; he
became so impoverished that it was found
necessary, after his death, to sell Sandringham and the adjoining manors, the possession
of his family for two hundred years.

Blomefield says, " This William was a
great royalist, and a colonel in the army or
militia, and suffered greatly on that account."

Playfair,* in describing him, mentions that
he was "particularly distinguished for his
exertions during the Civil Wars, and a severe
sufferer for his loyalty ;" a contemporary
document bears testimony that he was " in
arms against the Parliament," in 1643,† and

---

* " British Family Antiquity."   By William Playfair.
London, 1809.   A folio in nine volumes.

† "I do find by the several Returns from the county

one cause of the diminution of his fortune
was his contributing to the expenses of the
militia corps or trained band of which he
was colonel, as it is evident, from his name
not appearing in the army lists of the time,
that he was not in the regular army.

But it was not only as an active royalist,
in arms against the parliament, but also as a
Recusant and Papist that Colonel Cobbe suffered. His religious convictions, confessed by
himself in one of his letters, no less than his
political principles, brought distress and per-
plexity into the desolate old mansion standing
amid its lonely and wind-swept moors.

Strange although it seems, that Sandringham, the very spot, the very site, now so
prosperous and favoured, should have undergone such vicissitudes, and past through such
deep and bitter waters ; it is nevertheless true

of Norfolk that William Cobbe, of Sandringham, Esq.,
. . . . was a Recusant, and in arms against the Parliament." This refers to the year 1643, and is signed
R. J. Sherwin, and dated Sept. 9, 1652.—" Royalist
Composition Papers," vol. xv., p. 594.

that the estate was sequestrated for years, and that the owner, forbidden even to live within its denuded walls, gained no compensation whatever for the nine years of absolute penury when the income derived from his manors, which then extended, as now, into five parishes beyond Sandringham, was appropriated by the Roundheads.

The sequestration of the estates of Roman Catholic Royalists was one of the principal sources of revenue upon which the Commonwealth depended ; the ordinances for forfeiture were mercilessly executed ; and it must have given the crowning sting to misfortune, when the just owner of a landed property had to reflect that every farthing taken from him was expended in the struggle to enforce the tenets and policy that he abhorred.

The following letters, copied from the originals in the Public Record Office, give the facts of Colonel Cobbe's case,* and show that

---

* The letters quoted are bound up, and are in vol xv., pp. 529, 536, 585, 594, 605, 608, and in vol. xxxix.,

not only the customary two-thirds, but the whole of his possessions became forfeited. One of them, written by himself, to "the Honourable the Commissioners for managing my estates under sequestration," states that the "whole profit" of his estates "was for many years received for the use of the Commonwealth." The petitions are all addressed to the Commissioners for Compounding. The earliest is dated July 2, 1650, and is an appeal from two ruined tenants of " William Cobbe, of Sandringham, Esq., Papist and Delinquent."

The next two are from himself; one, dated November 7, 1650, — "Sheweth ; that the petitioner's estate is sequestered, albeit not any delinquency hath bin or can be proved against him, neither is he convicted of Recusancy, notwithstanding the commissioners for the sayd county [Norfolk] have sequestered him as a Recusant. He humbly praieth a

p. 197, of the first series of "Royalist Composition Papers."

F

discharge of the sayd sequestration on being a Recusant, tho' unconvicted, and that the commissioners would allow him a third of his estate with his mansion house.

"Signed WILLIAM COBBE."

Four days later he wrote, "The petitioner's estate is sequestered, albeit no proof is or can be made against him for delinquency, neither is he convicted of Recusancy, however he humbly confesseth his Recusancy, and humbly praieth the allowance of a third of his estate with the mansion house. November 11, 1650."

The next document relating to Colonel Cobbe is "a petition from the Lord Ambassador of the King of Spain on behalf of Colonel William Cobb, Esq."

"Ordered by the Parliament; that it be referred to the Commissioners for compounding to examine the state of the case of Colonel William Cobb, whose estate stands sequestered, and with all convenient speed certifie true state thereof to the Parliament. 30th July, 1651."

After several petitions from tenants on the estate comes a paper showing the difficulty of obtaining relief. The Commissioners for Compounding, finding that Colonel Cobbe had obtained an order for "his thirds and mansion house," in answer to his appeal of November, 1650, had refused to act upon it, "supposing he had obtained the order by some false suggestion." This report, made July 15th, 1652, was read November 3rd, 1652, as certified by Henry Scobell, Clerk to the Parliament, and, on the same day, his rights were restored to him, Wednesday, 3rd of November, 1652.*

"Resolved, upon the question by the Parliament, that the sequestration of William Cobbe of Sandringham, in the county of Norfolk, Esq., be discharged.

"Henry Scobell, Clerk, Parlt."

---

* Many of the possessions of Papists and delinquents, forfeited for the benefit of the Commonwealth, were re-

In the corner of this document :—

"John Pulford maketh oathe that he examined the copy with the original remayning with Henry Scobell, Clerk of the Parliament, and that it is a true copie of the Record.

"John Pulford, 16th November, 1652, R.M."

But the restitution was slow; six months later, Mary Cobb, "being very aged and infirm," an annuitant on the estate, prays that the Commissioners would be pleased to grant an order of allowance, the estate of William Cobb being now discharged from sequestration by order of Parliament.

Sandringham, in common with most other of the estates of "Papists and delinquents," was sequestered in 1643. The sequestration took place in September, "about Michaelmas," just after the siege of Lynn, when it is likely that Colonel Cobbe contributed to the

stored after seven years, and these first forfeitures were followed by hundreds of sequestrations of both real and personal property.

assistance sent to the garrison by the neighbouring country gentlemen.

That ever loyal town stood out bravely against the Duke of Manchester's forces, but capitulated at last.

Sir Hamon le Strange, and his son Roger, Sir Henry Bedingfeld, Sir Richard Hovell of Hillington, and others, went to the defence of Lynn, on horseback, they and their men armed with swords and pistols.

The documents at Hunstanton Hall, rich as they are in domestic records, fail to throw light on the event, in which the le Stranges were so closely concerned, the papers and letters relating to it having been, doubtless, purposely destroyed, as compromising; but a curious old narrative of the siege of Lynn, contained in a small pamphlet printed soon after by "G. Bishop and R. White,"* gives many particulars, and states that Sir Henry Bedingfeld was one of the hostages kept until

---

* Now in the possession of E. M. Beloe, Esq., of King's Lynn.

the conditions of the surrender had been fulfilled.

The life of Sir Henry Bedingfeld, the father of Mrs. Cobbe, was as melancholy as that of his son-in-law. He fought under the royal standard as soon as the civil war broke out, was taken prisoner, and committed to the Tower, as described by his son, Henry Bedingfeld, on a leaf of a manuscript volume at Oxburgh, "Meditations on the Passion of our Saviour." "This book was written with my dear father Sir Henry Bedingfeld's own hand, whilst he was a prisoner in the Tower, where he was one yeare and three quarters, and procured his release about Hollimas, 1649." It goes on to say, "his estate was sold over his head for delinquency, in the year '52; he departed this life, after many sufferings, the 22nd of November, 1656, having been ill of a quartan ague ten weeks; he was buried in Oxburgh Church, aged about seventy-five years and a half."

The writer was eventually the first baronet,

and another brother of Mrs. Cobbe's was Edmund, eminent for his piety, a canon of Lier, in Brabant, where he died.

Mrs. Cobbe had several children; over and over again was Sandringham, during the proprietorship of the Cobbes, peopled and enlivened by an enormous family of children. But these sociable times were to come to an end.

Geoffrey Cobbe, who inherited Sandringham in 1665, from his father, the royalist colonel, married Frances Astley, of Melton, and had an only child, Elizabeth. Geoffrey sold the lordship of Sandringham in or about 1686; his daughter was living in 1727, and gave particulars of the fate of the family to Mr. Le Neve.*

---

* Some of the particulars are printed in the "Visitation of Norfolk," where a note of Le Neve's is quoted: "All this I had from the information of Mrs. Elizabeth Cobb, anno 1727. P. L. Norroy." She was under sixty-two in 1727. Le Neve died two years afterwards. The account of Colonel Cobbe in Blomefield's "Norfolk" was presumably communicated from this source.

After the death of Colonel Cobbe the family dwindled away; of his four sons, two were priests, and the fourth left no children; he had five daughters, Elizabeth, Dorothy, Anne, Mary, and Frances; the first four took the veil in foreign convents, where they died.

The devotion to the royal cause, and the fidelity to the old faith, which had cost Colonel Cobbe so dear, dispersed his house, and Norfolk knew it no more; the large domestic circle which had inhabited Sandringham gradually drifted into obscurity in the cells beyond the sea.

> "For aye to be in shady cloister mewed,
> Chanting faint hymns to the cold fruitless moon."

There are some Cobbe pedigrees which were sent to the writer of this book by Mr. Edward Cobbe, of Bath, in 1883, and from which may be inferred the probability that the Cobbes of Hampshire, Norfolk, and Ireland had a common root. If so, the owners of the name possess a link with a famous Irish ghost story.

From Harper's Magazine.

There is a tombstone in Weston churchyard, near Bath, on which is inscribed :—
" The Right Hon. Lady Elizabeth Cobbe,
died May 6th, 1806, aged sixty-nine." Her
husband was Mr. Thomas Cobbe, of New-
bridge, in the County of Dublin, and died in
March, 1814, aged eighty-one.

On his death, the subject was revived, and
canvassed in the local contemporary news-
papers, of the mysterious occurrence which
had happened many years before to Lady
Beresford, the grandmother of Lady Elizabeth, or, as she is commonly called, Lady
Betty, Cobbe, when the apparition of the Earl
of Tyrone, immediately after his death, stood
by the bedside of his former friend and companion.

It was found, on the death of Mr. Cobbe,
that a piece of broad black riband concerned
with the story, had been carefully preserved
by Lady Betty, to whom it had been given
by her father. Lady Betty herself, who had
been in her youth, a prominent personage in

the fashionable world of Dublin, and celebrated for her wit and liveliness, firmly believed in the story, which she often narrated. She had not only come into possession of the black riband, but also of her grandmother's pocket book, in which was a mysterious autograph.

There is a manuscript in the possession of Lady Hamilton (the widow of Sir James John Hamilton, a descendant of the Beresfords), which is copied from one taken down from Lady Betty Cobbe's own lips, by the Honble. Mrs. Maitland, and which bears the date,—" Tellerig, July, 1794."

The manuscript gives, with much detail, the story that Lord Tyrone, and Nicola Hamilton, daughter of Lord Glenrawley, both orphans, were educated together in atheistical principles; that she married Sir Tristram Beresford, in 1687; that Lord Tyrone died in 1693, and then appeared to her, bearing his testimony to the truth of a future life, and clasping her wrist, which ever after bore a black mark, as a proof that his visit was a reality and not a dream; foretelling to her the birth of her son, her second marriage, and her death at the age of forty-eight.

An old lady now living, one of the Beresfords, relates that she remembers in early childhood, at Curraghmore, near Waterford, the old seat of the Beresfords, a chest of drawers, said to have been in the room when the ghost appeared.

It is clear that the belief in the truth of the story was unshaken on the part of the family as early as 1737, the year of Lady Betty's birth, a few years after Lady Beresford, on her deathbed, revealed the occurrence, which she had up to that time, kept secret.

Lady Betty was the daughter of Sir Marcus Beresford, the eldest son of Sir Tristram and Nicola Lady Beresford. Sir Marcus was created fourth Earl of Tyrone, having married the only child and heiress of James, third Earl of Tyrone, who had succeeded his brother,

John, second Earl. The families of Tyrone and Beresford were curiously mixed up, as the childish friend and subsequent spiritual visitor of Lady Beresford, was John, second Earl of Tyrone, the uncle (if ghosts can be uncles) of the heiress who married Lady Beresford's own son, which son, in his turn, became, in consequence, an Earl of Tyrone.

The popular printed accounts of the occurrence assert that Lady Betty received the story—hitherto concealed—from Nicola Lady Beresford herself, when she was dying, a month after the birth of a child by her second husband, Mr. Gorges, and that Lady Betty took the riband from her wrist ; but this assertion is an error, as proved by the dates on Lady Betty's tombstone, and the confession and the riband must have been conveyed to Lady Betty by her father, or by some person older than herself who had received them ; and there is just the possibility, although the existence of the black riband and other testimonies, make the rejection of the tale

more full of difficulties than the belief in it,
—that Lady Beresford, in the delirium of her
dying illness, may have imagined the whole
affair.

CHAPTER VIII.

THE STORY OF THE HOSTES.

AFTER an interval, Sandringham came into the hands of the Hostes, who occupied the old manor house about a hundred and twenty years, living altogether at Sandringham one hundred and fifty years.

The name of Hoste takes us away to the country to which the family belonged, and from whence it originally came to England,* and brings us once more to Bruges, where, for nearly two centuries, beginning from 1294, members of the family of Hoost are men-

---

* The remoter source of the Hoste family is said to identify it with the " Ostmen " of Scandinavia.

tioned in the records of the Town Hall, as taking a prominent part in the affairs of the municipality.

When the Anglo-Flemish alliance was at its height, in 1345, Jacques Hoost was a sheriff of Bruges, and was succeeded in that office during the subsequent seventy years by six of his name.

Towards the middle of the fifteenth century, the head of the family appears at Middleburg, in Zealand, whither it is surmised he had been driven by the opposition of Charles the Bold to the more important burghers of the Flemish towns. Others of the family remained at Bruges, where their descendants are still to be found.

In the midst of the governorship of the Duke of Alva, and the troublous times which accompanied it, a Jacques Hoost migrated from Middleburg to England, in one of the innumerable privateers which swarmed from every port on the winding coast of Holland, and which were destined to convey to England and Germany not only the noble families which had been exiled, but large numbers of merchants and skilled workmen who had been ruined at home, and who then transferred to their adopted countries the knowledge of commerce, the enterprise, and the industries which had made the greatness of their own fair and populous cities.

Jacques Hoost arrived in London in 1569 ; his wife was Barbara Henricks, the daughter of Theoderick Henricks. He received, on naturalization in England, the addition of wings to his coat of arms and a pair of wings for a crest, in allusion to his flight from Holland.

He settled in London as a merchant, and had a son, Theoderick, who flourished in the days of James I. and Charles I. ; a zealous Puritan, of whom there exists a fine portrait by Cornelis Jansen.

Theoderick's wife was Jane Desmastres, the daughter of a rich merchant; and his son James, who also married a London merchant's daughter, bought the estate at Sandringham shortly after 1686.

Among the objects contained in the two successive houses at Sandringham inhabited by the Hostes (as their name was spelt after their arrival in England) was a family picture representing a young girl who was burnt at the stake during the persecution of the Protestants by the Duke of Alva in the Netherlands. This picture is mentioned in Blomefield's " History of Norfolk."

In the account of Sandringham to be found there, the following sentence occurs after the statement of Jacques Hoost's flight from Middleburg to England :—" There is a curious picture here of a young lady of the family, burned in those times for her religion as a Protestant."

When Blomefield died in 1752, after completing three-fifths of his history, Mr. Parkin, of Oxburgh, continued it. His MS., and the notes and papers written by Blomefield, from which the latter made his final copy, are in the Bodleian library.   G

In Parkin's MS. the first part of the above sentence is written as a note at the foot of the page, and the second part is added in later ink, also in his handwriting. But in the original the words run: *not* "burned in those times for her religion, &c.;" but "burned in those at ye time for her religion as a Protestant."

Parkin intended to write "in those parts," or "in those countries," referring to his previous sentence describing the Hostes as "of Middleburg in Zealand," but omitted a word, and the compositor emended the sentence as well as he could. It is known that Parkin avoided correcting proofs, and that the labour of the publication rested with his publisher, Whittingham, of Lynn; hence the permanent error.

This testimony coincides with the unwritten tradition handed down in the family itself that the original of the portrait, and another of its members, were burned by order of the Duke of Alva during his administration in Flanders.

The picture was therefore at Sandringham in the last century, within two hundred years of the event it commemorates. It was there also in this century.

An inhabitant of the house in 1820, where the story of the Flemish martyr was a household word, describes it as a half-length portrait of a young lady standing up against a dark background; the face encircled by a stiff cap covered with fine lace, the dress a plain black gown of solid texture.

The picture was in a room called the "Kitchen Chamber," a bedroom over the kitchen, which contained a number of old Dutch portraits, apparently put there to be out of the way, piled against the wall in the unused room.

When Blomefield or Parkin saw it, it was in the "old manor-house;" in 1820 it was in the newly rebuilt house, which looked east, the iron front gates opening on to the Anmer road.

The servants in the house used to steal

up to the chamber thus strangely peopled, to gaze at the figure of the girl, her calm face and sombre dress lit up as the evening sunshine streamed into the room.

The picture is now in Somersetshire, in the possession of Colonel Henley, the representative of the elder branch of the Hostes of Sandringham. On it is written the age of the girl, "ætatis suæ 18;" but the name was not painted in, or has been erased.

The portrait was painted when the generation to which she belonged was passing away; it is without signature of artist. She holds a Bible in her hand, and this Bible, held as a sacred relic, with a veneration which "gilded refined gold," was kept by the Hostes for many generations, and has only been mislaid within the last few years.

It is possible that lists may exist at Bruges of some of those who were put to death during the years between 1567 and 1573, but the butchery was so extensive, and included so many of obscure rank and unknown name

—distinguished only in "the better resurrection"—that the fate of many individuals must remain unrecorded, who perished in the long struggle before the Netherlands rose serene, established, and triumphant, under the presidency of that patriotic line of champions, the Princes of Orange.

Motley tells us that the tens of thousands of victims "to the stake, the sword, the gallows, the living grave, have never been counted;" such barbarous statistics are too often wrapped in darkness; and this absence of evidence gives an unusual interest to any fragment which rescues one image at least out of the sea of upturned dying faces.

It is an abrupt contrast to turn from these harrowing events to the quiet scenes of Sandringham; yet they were entered upon by the same family scarcely a hundred years after its dire experiences in the Netherlands.

James Hoste, the purchaser of the estate, began life in London, but lived at or near Sandringham before the place belonged to him, as appears by the entries of the births of his children in the register.

The first occurs in 1677, nine years before Geoffrey Cobbe relinquished the property.

Mr. Hoste was succeeded by a son, the second James Hoste of Sandringham, whose first wife, Elizabeth, daughter of Sir Edward Walpole, of Houghton, died early without leaving children; his second wife was Ann Burleigh.

Their eldest son, James, married Susan Hamond of Wooton, and inherited Sandring-ham; from the second son, Theodore, de-scended Sir William Hoste, well known in naval history. The elder line was continued, after James Hoste and Susan Hamond, by an only surviving child, Susan, heiress of Sandringham, who, in August, 1752, married Mr. Cornish Henley, of Leigh House, in Somersetshire.

Mr. and Mrs. Henley lived exclusively at Sandringham, in the manor-house; if inscrip-tions on tombstones and family portraits can be trusted, she was a benevolent, popular, and good-looking châtelaine. She survived her husband, and died in 1795, leaving a son, Henry Hoste Henley, in possession of Sandringham.

Theodore, the second son of James Hoste and Ann Burleigh, migrated from Sandringham to Ingoldisthorpe Hall, also in Norfolk. He was the father of the Reverend Dixon Hoste, whose son William was created a baronet for his services in the Peninsular war.

William Hoste was a favourite, and, although much younger, almost a friend of Nelson, under whom he first went to sea in 1793.

Nelson, in one of his letters, written when William Hoste was only seventeen years old, prophesied that he would be an honour to Norfolk and England, and his career justified this opinion. He was present at the battle of the Nile, where, for his gallant conduct, he was given the command of a brig, and sent to Gibraltar to announce the joyful victory.

Eight days before the battle of Trafalgar he was appointed by Nelson to the *Amphion,* but missed that glorious occasion. "Not to have been in it, is enough to make one mad," he writes; "I am low indeed, and nothing but a good action with a French or Spanish frigate will set me up again."

He then joined Admiral Collingwood, "a very different man from Lord Nelson, but as brave an old boy as ever lived." The most distinguished exploit of Captain Hoste was that of March, 1811, when commanding a squadron of four frigates in the Gulf of Venice. Beneath the mountains of Lissa, the island which rises from the centre of the Adriatic, he met the French and Venetian squadron, doubling his own in the number of vessels, and with three times the number of men. Just before the English ships opened fire, Captain Hoste telegraphed the signal,— "Remember Nelson." The English sailors rose to the thrilling watchword, and in six hours the action was over and the victory won.

From Harper's Magazine.

Copyright, 1886, by Harper & Brothers.

THE PRINCESS DRIVING PAST "ALEXANDRA COTTAGES," BUILT BY THE PRINCE (*page* 25).

If Jacques Hoste augmented his coat-of-arms by two wings, in memorial of his flight across the German Ocean, Sir William Hoste, his descendant, earned the right to engrave two words upon his,—"Lissa" and "Cattaro," —both of which certainly signified something very different from flight. In the capture of Cattaro, the almost inaccessible fortress which frowned down upon the Adriatic from the hills of Montenegro, he added another page to the story of his brief but brilliant days of service. His health had been damaged by the hardships and accidents of sea warfare, and he died at the age of forty-eight, in 1828.

During this time the family house at Sandringham had undergone great changes. Mr. Hoste Henley had taken much of it down, and had made additions, constituting almost a new edifice.

A long low house, with wings, and rather small windows; the staircase, forgotten in the alterations, awkwardly penetrating the roof of the hall. One of the rooms was lined with a large collection of shells, and occupied by a company of stuffed bears, lions, and tigers; in another were some genre pictures and curious volumes, among them French illuminated books.

When Sandringham was sold, on the death of Mr. Hoste Henley, in 1834, an auction took place, which dispersed, with the exception of the family pictures, these miscellaneous collections and the rest of the household furniture, among the neighbouring halls and rectories.

CHAPTER IX.

THE HUGUENOT FAMILY OF MOTTEUX.

AFTER the contents of the house had been removed, and the last waggon-wheels, "low on the sand, and loud on the stone," had finally echoed away, the place was relinquished to its new owner, whose name, difficult now to find in England, was known in London at the end of the seventeenth century, as that of a family of French refugees who had come over from Normandy at the time of the revocation of the edict of Nantes.

It thus befell that Sandringham, on two successive occasions, passed into the hands of a race whom religious persecution had

driven from foreign shores; the history of
these two families, as that of the Cobbes and
Walpoles, who suffered by means of a similar
cause, appears, on the face of it, to show how
strong the vitality of Christian faith, how
dominant the spiritual and sentimental side of
our nature, in the two centuries when they
endured and died; but the sufferings then
undergone in Holland, France, and England
were inflicted by Christians upon Christians,
for the sake of variation of opinion, and the
eternal battle between Catholic and Puritan,
Conformist and Nonconformist, in which men
and women cheerfully met death, had, and
has, in it also much of another very human
element, that of political opposition.

There lived at Rouen, in the latter half of
the seventeenth century, a thriving merchant,
called Antoine le Motteux.   When the edict
which had so long protected religious freedom
in France was revoked, several of his family,
rather than conform to Roman Catholicism,
left their rich and smiling province, their beau-

tiful and thriving town, and with these their
earthly prosperity, to take refuge in London.

England, under William III., afforded a
hospitable welcome to the French Huguenots;
their varied attainments, their industry, their
gentleness, their misfortunes, won them friends;
but his predecessor, with characteristic pre-
judice, looked upon these distressed beings,
—who made their way across the Channel
with hardship and difficulty, some tossed in
open boats, others disguised, some, like the
father of Dr. Barbauld, concealed doubled up
in a cask,—with an unfriendly eye.

Evelyn, in his journal, under the date of
November 3rd, 1685, in describing the immi-
gration, mentions that all the usual "passages"
from France were strictly guarded by sea
and land. He comments on the uncharitable
indifference of James II., and the fact that
the gazettes printed twice a week, "informing
us what was done all over Europe, never
spake of this wonderful proceeding in France,
nor was any relation of it published by any

save what private letters and the persecuted fugitives brought."

The grants for naturalizing these foreigners were slowly made, and hard to obtain; the country was reluctant to pass an Act for the purpose; it was not until Anne had been some years on the throne that a Bill, soon repealed, was passed.

Meanwhile, naturalization was dealt out to individuals by letters patent from the crown, the result being that the time of such grant was often deferred, and the date fails to stamp the moment of a refugees' arrival.

The adulatory tone adopted towards William and Mary in some of the poems of Pierre Antoine Motteux, the dramatist and translator of Rabelais, and one of the refugees, has been commented up; but it was neither common loyalty nor common flattery; eulogy couched in somewhat warmer terms than even the fulsome style of the day dictated, is not to be wondered at, when it is remembered what beneficent friends both had shown themselves to the refugees. William, who owed much to the Huguenot contingent which had joined his army, not only protected them, but promoted their endeavours to gain a livelihood.

"We do hereby declare, that all French Protestants that shall seek their refuge in this our kingdom, shall not only have our royal protection for themselves, families, and estates, within this our realm, but we will also do our endeavour in all reasonable ways and means so to support, aid, and assist them in their several and respective trades and ways of livelihood, as that their living and being in this realm shall be comfortable and easy to them. At the Court at Whitehall, 25th April, 1689."*

In the east of London, close to Victoria Park, stands the French Hospice, which has succeeded the building erected in 1718 for the reception of the aged poor among the Huguenot immigrants, and also as a rendezvous for those, who, needing immediate suc-

* Declaration issued by the king and queen.

cour, and a place for consultation and meeting, learned to know the hospice under the consoling name of "La Providence."

John Motteux, in 1729, was a director of this institution; Pierre Motteux, a director in 1759, and John, in 1763, The family thus kept up its connexion with the descendants of other refugees; the directors, as well as the governor, and other officers, having been, from the foundation of the institution until the present day, almost without exception, representatives of French Protestant refugee families, while the sole claim of an inmate to admission is the proof of such descent.

The Huguenot asylum was at the first in the parish of St. Luke, near the northern outskirts of London; a building three sides of a square, with numerous small windows, looking on to the pleasant lawns which surrounded it. This house has lately been pulled down, and a more modern one adorns a fresh spot.

So greatly have many of the Huguenots prospered in the last hundred and fifty years, that the hospice has been endowed and supported solely by members of these distinguished and interesting families.

The hospice is too little known, chiefly from the refreshing contrast it presents to the institutions whose existence depends upon their incessant appeals to the public.

"Rich and poor have here met together;" all of one mind; the first to give, the latter to receive, the benefits of a healthful home, replete with refinement and comfort. Indeed, so all-sufficient have the funds proved that the directors in 1881—when the Lord Mayor of London was entertained at dinner in their spacious "court-room," and desired to leave a substantial gift to the refuge he so much admired—declined the money, and compromised by accepting a pair of ravens, in allusion to the badge of the hospice—the ravens feeding the prophet Elijah.

These birds—ravens being apparently more blessed in giving than in receiving—both came to a distressing end, and the best parts remaining of the two were united to form the one stuffed specimen which sits, motionless and typical, watching the consumption of bread and flesh in the dining-hall beneath.*

> "Say, pitying mortal, would it be so hard a fate,
> When death has claim'd both you and your dear mate,
> That all the best of both, in one fond memory blended,
> Should live—and in forgetfulness all else be ended?"

It was in the beginning of James the Second's reign that the Motteuxes left Rouen, and arrived in the east of London. A list of Huguenot refugees, made in 1685, gives the names of several children of Antoine le Motteux; † among them, Pierre Antoine; and the name of John Motteux, and those of John Anthony, Peter, and Timothy, his sons, occur in the list containing names of persons born

---

* The Hospice contains sixty inmates, men and women. It is desired to befriend a class of superior birth and education, always observing the necessary condition, and arrangements are being made to group together educated persons whose broken health or age precludes them from continuing their vocation as governesses or teachers.

† This is mentioned by M. Haag, in "La France Protestante," 1860, vols. vii., viii., p. 550.

"in partibus transmarinus," naturalized by royal letters patent, Westminster, under April 15, 1693.*

John Motteux was the elder brother of Pierre Antoine. From John, the late Mr. John Motteux, of Sandringham, was lineally descended. †

The name of Motteux appears from time to time during the last century in contemporary records and notices, mainly in connexion with the efforts made by the more prosperous Huguenots, among whom they held a high position, for their poorer brethren.

John Anthony Motteux, the earliest director of the name, was the first-mentioned child on the list of 1693, a grandson of Antoine le Motteux, of Rouen. The death

---

* A folio volume was published in 1861, by the Rev. David Agnew, "Protestant Exiles from France," in which lists are given during the reigns of Charles II., James II., and William and Mary, copied afresh by himself from the Patent Rolls. A more limited set of lists was published by the Camden Society.

† See Motteux Pedigree, Appendix B.

of the director is recorded in the *Gentleman's Magazine*, "December 26, 1741.—Mr. John Motteux, an eminent Hamburgh merchant," and his burial is entered in the register of St. Andrew Undershaft Church, in the Parish of St. Mary Axe, "January the 1st, 1742." The other two directors of the name were his nephew, and his son, John Motteux, of Walbrook, London, and Beachamwell, in Norfolk.

Pierre Antoine, a son of the Rouen merchant, is, as a writer of some distinction, the best known of the name. He was twenty-five years of age when he emigrated from Rouen, in 1685, and the remainder of his life was spent in London. Although he never appears to have been in the position of those fellow-authors who must "starve or sing," his productions were numerous.

He was a writer of English plays and poems, but pre-eminently a translator, and excelled in this branch of literature rather than the former, not only from his command of languages, but from his power of entering into the temperament of a favourite author, and reproducing his peculiar impressions.

Motteux had the impulse to write himself, but his versions of the works of Rabelais and Cervantes, writers with whom his own qualities claimed some kinship, have survived him, and become classics, whilst his plays, coarse and dull, although praised in poetic epistle by Dryden, are forgotten.

In the second of Hogarth's series, "The four times of the day," which is called "Noon," the painter has taken for his subject a congregation of people coming out of the French Protestant chapel in "Hog Lane." In the distance is the church of St. Giles, with the hands of the clock not far from twelve; in the foreground, turning both ways, the slightly-grotesque persons, old, young, and middle-aged, who are streaming off home across the dirty street.

The figure of the smart, talkative, flippant-looking gentleman, who advances with a lively step, was painted some years after the death of Pierre Antoine Motteux, but it gives his type, a type which had become commoner when Hogarth satirized Frenchmen, than in the first days when the earliest French strangers cherished the flame of their pure faith in the plain rooms and dusty plaistered walls which served as chapels, bearing on their faces the serious and noble stamp of recent suffering and resolve.

Family example, intolerance of oppression, desired scope for a literary career, sent Pierre Antoine to London, but from the pathetic glory which a stern romance sheds over his fellow-exiles, he is altogether free. It is an unexpected fact how completely all allusion to his experience at Rouen of the persecutions of "the patient Huguenot" is absent from his works or letters.

But, although thus separate from his traditions, he had the Huguenot characteristics of intelligence and industry, and possessed a character useful, enterprising, and capable.

After being well educated at Rouen, where

he was born, in February, 1660, he lived, on
first coming to England, with a relation, Paul
Dominique, a merchant in the city. He soon
showed the mercantile ability and business
habits which enabled him to achieve a high
position himself in trade, keeping a large East
India warehouse in Leadenhall Street—and,
in addition to this, he held for some time a
situation in the foreign department of the
Post Office.

But he had leisure for other pursuits; his
love of conversation is alluded to by Pope :—

> "At last Centlivre felt her voice to fail,
> Motteux himself unfinish'd left his tale." *

> " Talkers I've learn'd to bear ; Motteux I knew,
> Henley himself I've heard, and Budgel too." †

His facility in acquiring languages is proved,
for, although he lived in Normandy the first
half of his life, his skill in the English language, and freedom from foreign idiom, ranked
him as an English writer even in the days of

---

* Dunciad, book ii., verse 411.
† Satire of Donne, versified, sat. iv., line 50.

Swift, Steele, and Addison ; an unusual proficiency which was due to his associating solely with Londoners, instead of with his fellow-refugees.

Although he abjured the jovial drinking habits of the day, and, judging by his poem on tea, and other indications, was a " total abstainer," he was given to indulgences more questionable still, and, in spite of a beautiful wife and a family of young children, his morals had none of the austerity of his Huguenot training, but were of the most easy-going description.

Literature, trade, and pleasure filled up a life which was busy and merry enough, but ended somewhat prematurely and suddenly, and not very creditably, when he was out one night in London amusing himself in a long scarlet cloak, hat, and sword, driving about in a hackney coach, to the distress and anxiety of Priscilla Motteux, his wife, who sat at home in Leadenhall Street, awaiting the return of the " China man," as he was called in the City.

The China man was being murdered, and his death, on his fifty-eighth birthday, caused some sensation, and occupied the journals of the day, but his fate, and that of his murderers, cannot be clearly gathered from these sources.

The story, as narrated by the late Mr. John Motteux to a friend in Norfolk, was, that Peter Anthony (as he came to be called) was hanged up in sport, and that a procession passing in the street, his companions ran to the window to look at it, and, before they returned, he was dead. He was buried in the church of St. Andrew Undershaft : " Peter Anthony Motteux, Feb. 22, 1717."

The births of two of his sons, Anthony and Francis, born respectively in 1705 and 1710, are also there registered. His will contains the most affectionate expressions towards his wife and children, whom he left well provided for, and contains bequests to the poor of the parish.

CHAPTER X.

LITERARY REMAINS OF PETER ANTHONY MOT-
TEUX—JOHN MOTTEUX, OF SANDRINGHAM.

ETER ANTHONY MOT-
TEUX'S translation of the
works of Rabelais, which
takes rank as the best that exists—
pronounced by Tytler in his essay on
Translation to be "one of the most
perfect specimens of translation"—
was brought out in 1694; the first
three books being a revision of a previous
version by other hands, the remaining three
Motteux's direct interpretation from the
French.

The preface which he wrote to these volumes has been translated into French, and

occupies a recognized niche in French literature. The explanations which he offers of the allegories, although now superseded, are, as well as his judicious remarks on the character of François Rabelais, written in remarkably clear and well-selected English.

Soon after this publication he began to write plays, which were acted at the Lincoln's Inn Fields theatre. One of them, " Beauty in Distress," published in 1698, was preceded by a poem addressed to Motteux by Dryden. It begins with an allusion to the vocation of a dramatist, as compared with that of other teachers :—

" The moral part at least we may divide.
    Humility reward, and punish pride;
    Ambition, interest, avarice, accuse,
    These are the province of the tragic muse.
    These hast thou chosen, and the public voice
    Has equall'd thy performance with thy choice;
    Time, action, place, are so preserved by thee,
    That even Corneille might with envy see
    The alliance of his tripled unity.
    Let thy own Gauls condemn thee, if they dare,
    Born there, but not for them, our fruitful soil
    With more increase rewards thy happy toil.

It moves our wonder that a foreign guest,
Should overmatch the most, and match the best.
Words, once my stock, are wanting to commend,
So great a poet, and so good a friend."

This tragedy proved a success. Motteux
was fortunate enough to bring it out at a
moment when one of the most popular
actresses of the day was ready to present the
sorrows and triumphs of the heroine Placentia
in the antechamber at Lisbon, with all the
skill, grace, and animation required to embellish the part.

There is a small print of Mrs. Bracegirdle,
which echoes feebly the bright descriptions
given of her by contemporary writers. Even
in the dull old print the large dark eyes and
marked eyebrows show what power these
must in reality have given to the face. The
hair is drawn up in shining masses, the mouth,
like Cupid's bow, pouting and expressive; the
figure beautifully moulded, in a loose white
dress, which falls away and shows the throat
and neck.

"She was of a lovely height, with dark

brown hair and eyebrows, black sparkling eyes, and a fresh blushy complexion; and whenever she exerted herself, had an involuntary flushing in her breast, neck, and face, having continually a cheerful aspect, and a fine set of even white teeth." *

Colley Cibber describes her as "a brunette, with such a lovely aspect and such a glow of health and cheerfulness in her countenance, that she inspired everybody with love. Scarce an audience saw her that were not half of them her lovers, without a suspected favourite among them." †

Cibber's further sketch of Mrs. Bracegirdle bears out the popular belief—held in spite of the few who grudged to an actress, in all the bloom of her youth and beauty, and in those lenient days, the power to remain in the narrow path of virtue—that she was guarded in

* Anthony Aston's supplement to Cibber's account, in Genest's "History of the Stage," under "Lincoln's Inn Fields Theatre."

† In Cibber's "Apology for My Life."

her private character, and preserved an untarnished reputation. Even Congreve, to whom she gave much of her company and a large share of her heart, sang his passion and its hopelessness in the impatient lines :—

> " Pious Celinda goes to prayers,
>   Whene'er I ask a favour ;
> Yet the tender fool's in tears,
>   When she believes I'll leave her.
> Would I were free from the restraint,
>   Or else had power to win her,
> Would she could make of me a saint,
>   Or I of her a sinner."

Like Peg Woffington, who consoled the indigent with gifts and gaiety, putting down her basket of loaves on the bare table and dancing a gavotte on the still barer floor, Mrs. Bracegirdle was given to be charitable, and was well known and beloved in a locality called Clare Market, where she relieved the unemployed basket-women, and could not pass that neighbourhood without the thankful acclamations of the inhabitants.

But while her excellent personations of the heroines of genteel comedy were still in all their popularity, the wheel went on turning, and another actress came up. Mrs. Oldfield appeared, and Mrs. Bracegirdle, unwilling to risk the inconstancy of the public, left the stage, and after February, 1707, her name does not appear in the bills.

The remnants of "charming Bracegirdle" were occasionally seen in the Strand, near which she lived; and one Sunday night in September, 1748, her coffin was taken from Howard Street, and laid in the cloisters of Westminster Abbey.

Motteux was never so brilliantly represented again as during the run of "Beauty in Distress." After this play he wrote musical interludes and masques ; among others, "Acis and Galatea," which was represented with musical accompaniment, preceding by some years the more celebrated version by Gay and Handel.

In 1700 he published his translation of "Don Quixote," made direct from the Spanish. The numerous editions which have followed

one another, from its first issue up to the
present time, testify to the success of this
work; the early editions, "adorned with
sculptures," were in four books, each book
dedicated to a separate patron; the second
to Mr. Edward Coke, of Holkham. Motteux's
dedication, after the usual amount of flattery,
alludes, with just appreciation, to the "charming and virtuous partner" of Mr. Coke.

This was Carey Newton, a fair and accom-
plished woman, the worthy mother of an only
son, the first Earl of Leicester, distinguished
like herself for a true and delicate taste in
literature and art.

The tall, graceful figure, the fine intelligent
aspect of this lady, have been handed down
in two portraits at Holkham. Her bright
dark eyes and slender fingers were prone to
peruse and turn the leaves of choice and
dainty volumes.

These she collected, and enriched with
her own individual book plate. One of
these little labels, which are so convenient in

emphasizing present ownership, and so interesting as recording past possessors, is to be
found beneath the cover of the first of four
octavo volumes, containing Peter Anthony
Motteux's History of Don Quixote, which
Carey Coke added to the library at Holkham,—

"Carey Coke, wife of Edward Coke, of Norfolk, Esq.,
1701."

There is a letter contributed by Motteux
to the *Spectator* for January 30, 1711-12,
which, though intended as a satire upon
tradesmen's puffs, is an acknowledgment from
his own pen of his mercantile enterprises,
his literary works, and his habitation.

He alludes to "the books I translated—
'Rabelais' and 'Don Quixote,'" and to the
warehouse in Leadenhall Street, near the
India Company, where he displayed wares
from China and Japan, pictures, tea, fans,
muslins, gold and silver brocades, and foreign
silks, for the fair customers who graced his
rooms. The shop was called "The Two

I

Fans," and was a well-known fashionable rendezvous.

The mention of pictures explains the letter now in the British Museum, torn, yellow, and brittle, addressed by him to an " Honoured Doctor ——," enclosing a catalogue of pictures, "right originals," which he had to sell. The letter alludes to his private house in Leadenhall Street.

It is possible that Motteux's poem in praise of tea was also used as an advertisement, as it was published in 1712, but it appears too good for the purpose :—

"I saw the gods and goddesses above
Profusely feasting with imperial Jove;
The banquet done, swift round the nectar flew,
All Heaven was warm'd, and Bacchus boisterous grew,
Fair Hebe then the grateful Tea prepares,
Which to the feasting goddesses she bears.
The heavenly guests advance with eager haste,
They gaze, they smell, they drink, and bless the taste.
Refresh'd and charm'd, while thus employ'd, they sit,
More bright their looks, and more divine their wit.
'None,' says the god, 'shall with that tree compare,
Health, vigour, pleasure, bloom for ever there.
Sense for the learned, and beauty for the fair;

Hence, then, ye plants, that challenged once our praise,
The oak, the vine, the olive, and the bay;
No more let roses Flora's brow adorn,
Nor Ceres boast her golden ears of corn,
The Queen of Love her myrtles shall despise,
Tea claims at once the beauteous and the wise.
There, chemists, there your grand elixir see,
The panacea you should boast is Tea.
There, sons of art, your wishes doubled find,
Tea cures at once the body and the mind;
Chaste, yet not cold; and sprightly, yet not wild;
Tho' gentle, strong, and tho' compulsive, mild;
Fond Nature's paradox, that cools and warms,
Cheers without sleep, and tho' a medicine, charms.
Immortals, hear,' said Jove, ' and cease to jar;
Tea must succeed to wine, as peace to war;
Nor by the grape let men be set at odds,
But share in Tea the nectar of the gods.'"

Whatever may have been the literary merit of Peter Anthony Motteux, it is pleasant to turn aside from a picture, which, although displaying much that is genuine and brilliant, is yet bedaubed with some unwholesome hues, and contemplate his more sober successors in the family annals.

The last of these was Mr. John Motteux, of Beachamwell, near Swaffham, in Norfolk, and of Sandringham, great-great-nephew to this falling star, which so suddenly went out in darkness. His father, who bought Beach-amwell, in 1780, is buried there :—" John Motteux, Esq., of this parish, and of Banstead Place, in Surrey, who died on the 30th of April, 1793, aged 56 years."

The villagers long remembered the funeral, which was described by a very old man some few years ago as " gorgeous." It must have been gorgeous indeed, for the adjectives of the Norfolk rustic are, as a rule, below the mark, and unduly temperate.

He who was then buried was the son of John Anthony Motteux; and, besides Mr. John Motteux, of Sandringham, he had another son, Robert, who inherited Banstead. His London house, in Walbrook, was left to his sons, as also the capital of his business in the city, with directions for carrying on the firm.

Robert, and two daughters, were to inherit fortunes, the first of 20,000*l.*, the two latter of

PORTRAIT, FORMERLY AT SANDRINGHAM, OF A MEMBER OF THE
HOSTE FAMILY, BURNED AT THE STAKE (*page* 97).

15,000*l.* each. Robert and his sisters died
before their brother, and the late Mr. John
Motteux, who succeeded to the estate at
Beachamwell, on the death of his father,
when he was twenty-seven years old, started
in life with a fortune already made, which he
afterwards much increased by army contracts
during the early years of this century.

Sandringham and the adjacent property
happening to be in the market, he bought
the place as an investment merely, and never
lived there, occupying his house at Beachamwell, or that at Banstead, near Epsom.

He was alone in the world as to near relations, and a bachelor, but much in its society,
and possessing many friends. His French
extraction was well known. He went by the
name of "the little Huguenot," and himself
told the late Mr. Edward Ellice of his relationship to Peter Anthony Motteux.

A short man, rather stout, with large grey
whiskers, a commonplace manner, and most
unideal aspect, but whose dry remarks and

good humour are remembered at Beachamwell, where he entertained large shooting-
parties, filling the hall with guests. On these
occasions he would order the school, which he
had himself built and endowed, to be emp-
tied, and the children to be distributed about,
to brush the coverts, like so many spaniels;
afterwards, at the close of the day, they were
well recompensed for their dangerous frolic.
Those were other days, and schools were other
schools, and such things can only be whispered
in this responsible generation.

But his principal occupation was paying
visits; he was a frequent guest at the houses
of the Earl of Leicester and Earl Cowper, at
Woburn and at Holland House. A man was
naturally welcome who, on an approaching
marriage, would produce from his pocket, and
throw down on to the table, a fragment of
silver paper, containing unset diamonds of
great value as a wedding present; and his
conversation amused those who, like himself,
took an anxious interest in the flavour of their
wines and the confection of their dishes.

Mr. Hayward records a dispute which took place at Holland House between Lady Holland and Mr. Motteux,* when the revelation of an interesting political secret was checked by a warm discussion as to whether prunes should or should not be an ingredient in cock-a-leekie soup, Mr. Motteux maintaining that they were necessary. In fact, both were right; the three bunches of leeks, which give the requisite aroma to the stewed and peppered fowl swimming in broth, should be its only relish ; but when the leeks are meant to flavour veal soup, also called "cock-a-leekie," two dozen French plums must be thrown in, on the principle practised by Dr. Johnson :—

"A good veal pie well stuffed with plums,
  Was wondrous grateful to the doctor's gums."

Mr. Motteux kept a French cook; one of these gambled away the money entrusted to him for discharging the tradesmen's accounts, and committed suicide; another unfortunate

---

* Essay on Holland House, where the dispute only is mentioned.

cook was suddenly. taken ill on the morning
of a day when the house at Beachamwell was
filled with a large shooting-party ; Mr. Motteux, who had sent post-haste for the doctor,
addressed the latter thus :—" Bolster him up
for a few hours *till the dinner is served*, and
then let him die as soon as he likes ! "

Yet he was popular among his servants,
and among the poor around him, who profited
by his generosity and openhandedness; a
third cook received, in common with many
other persons whom he employed in various
departments, a handsome legacy and a pro-
vision for life.

When Mr. Motteux was in London, occupying one of the two houses he possessed
there, he occasionally met M. de Talleyrand,
who, during his visits to England, was the
constant guest of Lord and Lady Cowper.

After they had dined together one day at
Lord Cowper's house, Talleyrand (who had
been delighted during dinner with the English fashion of scooping out the contents of

marrow-bones, and, holding the bone upright in his left hand, had eaten the contents like soup with a spoon) turned to Lady Cowper and asked curiously, "Qui est donc ce petit monsieur qui a la manie des poires?" Mr. Motteux was discoursing on his usual topics, and French pears were at that moment in the ascendant.

The cultivation of these was a favourite hobby; at Sandringham he planted many of those picturesquely-growing trees which adorn with their silver blossom and gigantic golden pendants, the venerable domestic walls, the blooming orchards, the verdant gardens of his native Normandy. At Beachamwell, a fig, which he covered in with glass, was celebrated for its luxuriance and fertility; in that neighbourhood he studded the bleak uplands with plantations, and was proud of a handsome well-grown sycamore, which he planted on the village green, and which is still flourishing there.

But "sun and sky and breeze, and the

greenness of fields, and the delicious juices of meats and fishes, and society, and the cheerful glass, and candlelight, and fireside conversations, and jests, went out with life "* at last.

Dr. Johnson has said, " A man who is careless of his table is careless of other matters."

The converse was true of Mr. Motteux, who had so carefully managed his affairs, that, at his death, in July, 1843, he was in a position to leave a large fortune to his selected heir, and perhaps his long life of seventy-seven years, during which he took no medicine, and no corrective but lemon-juice, owed something to the recognition of the importance of careful cookery.

It may be remarked, in passing, of that very necessary industry, that, while its materials, drawn from the many kingdoms of the world of nature, and offering a million fairy flavours—and, still more, the delicacy and hazard of the operations which produce perfection of result—constitute it an art which

---

* Charles Lamb, " Essays of Elia."

can rise to the poetic, it is made unblest only by the estimable English matron, who complacently orders dinner in calm ignorance of the relative effects of the successive dishes which she rams into her family, by the mindless cook who supposes that we eat only to be filled, or the unskilful housewife, who turns the hardly-earned meat and flour into shoe-leather and poultices.

CHAPTER XI.

THE COUNTESS D'ORSAY.

N Mr. Motteux's time, Sandringham was unfurnished; it remained for his successor to make the house again habitable, the place " where once the garden smiled " cheerful with terrace, lawn, and flower-bed.

Some few days had elapsed after John Motteux had breathed his last in his house in Gloucester Place, when the door of a room under Lord Palmerston's roof, in Carlton House Terrace was gently opened one morning, and the silver tones of Lady Palmerston's voice wer: heard, announcing to its occupants that the possessions of the departed had been left to one of the family circle.

The Hon. Spencer Cowper was the third son of Lady Palmerston's first marriage, and at the time of the bequest was Secretary of Legation at Stockholm. He and his wife, Lady Harriet Cowper, spent some months of every year at Sandringham, from the time of their marriage in 1852, until it passed out of his possession ten years later.

Lady Harriet Cowper left some traces of her frequent residence there, and of the active benevolence which was the final phase of a life marked by unusual vicissitude. Her story had been throughout singular and pathetic, and a brief allusion to it is requisite to present her truly, as she appeared at Sandringham.

She was the only legitimate daughter of the first Earl of Blessington, and was born in 1812; her mother was a Scotchwoman, who died two years after her birth.

Her stepmother, celebrated for her fascinations, her powers of conversation, her contributions to a light fashionable literature, although credited with plenty of Irish warmth and good-humour, treated her with heartlessness ; her father, from whom she was much separated in her childhood, with a fatal want of consideration.

Lord and Lady Blessington, both Irish, lived first in London, and in 1822 went to Italy, accompanied by that many-gifted and misguided genius, Count Alfred d'Orsay. They lived in Italy many years, leaving Lady Harriet Gardiner in Dublin, under the care of an aunt.

On the death of Lord Blessington's son and heir—a child also left in Ireland—an arrangement was made, dated at Genoa, in 1823, by which one of the daughters was to marry Count d'Orsay, and inherit a part of Lord Blessington's Irish estates. Lady Harriet was selected.

The scheme had, therefore, been formed four years before its fulfilment in 1827, when Lady Harriet, aged fifteen years and four months, was taken from school in Dublin, and brought to Italy to be married to Count d'Orsay, whom she had never seen, and who was domiciled in her father's house.

The marriage took place at Naples, in December, a marriage only in name; the child appeared to be a mere pretext for the Count's continued presence in the family; she became reserved, soured, and unhappy, and is remembered shortly afterwards as sitting at one end of the drawing-room in Lord Blessington's house in Rome, dressed in a pinafore, and consigned to the companionship of her governess.

She describes, in the preface to one of her novels, " L'Ombre du Bonheur," the friendless condition which followed. " I was left alone in the wide world at twenty years of age, without the blessings of a family, and without any direct objects to which my affections might be legitimately attached. Silent and reserved, it was a constant consolation to me to confide my inmost thoughts to the guardianship of paper, instead of communicating them to those every-day acquaintances, miscalled friends.

The lonely life to which she refers commenced after her father's death. The Countess d'Orsay had accompanied Lord and Lady Blessington and Count d'Orsay to Paris, in 1829, and when Lord Blessington died, went to London with the two latter.

But, after a short time, she returned to Paris alone, and lived principally there from 1832, occupying herself in writing the novels and "feuilletons" in French, which afterwards gave place to the commentaries on the Scriptures, which she issued in the same language.

She had become a very beautiful woman, with a sensitive, poetical, and passionate nature, and unselfish heart; and with a mind highly cultivated by study, and by contact with the cream of a society at once socially and intellectually aristocratic. But, from a lack of power of thought and imagination, she seemed incapable of grasping wide views; the stamp of ability and force was absent; yet there was an air of reflection, and expression of composure about the fine chiselled features, and an influence which made itself felt in the tones of her especially rich and penetrating voice.

All this time she was not only neglected, but ignored by the man with whom she had been forced into such unholy bonds of matrimony,—that bald ceremony of a day long passed away, which had been gone through without choice, without intention, without heart, and, it might almost be said, without obligation.

That she should have yielded to the opportunity of forming a warm friendship during her life in Paris, can scarcely be judged severely, although there were those who condemned it. It is no wonder that compassion and friendship should have been lavished on the wife who was no wife, the woman who was so richly gifted a companion, while the character and position of the Duke of Orleans

K

obviously fitted him to dispense the sheltering kindness which could not have been otherwise than thankfully received by one in so desolate and peculiar a situation.

After the tragic death of the Duke, in July, 1842, the Countess d'Orsay remained in deep seclusion for some time, and on the death of Count Alfred d'Orsay, she became the wife of Mr. Spencer Cowper.

But a startling affliction awaited her. When the cholera broke out in Paris, in 1854, she was there with her husband and little daughter, an only child, two years old; a noble child, upright and rosy, with a crown of bright curls.

This baby, one day in September, showed slight symptoms of illness. Thinking that sea air might check the progress of disease, the parents set out with her for Dieppe. But the measure was useless; she was taken there only to die.

A morning or two after their arrival, as the first dawning streak of day floated through the windows, the child, throwing off her lethargy, broke "into voice a moment, then was still."

The furniture of the room in the Hotel at Dieppe, where she died, was transferred to Sandringham, where every article that had surrounded her, and the bed in which the little form had lain, were placed in a room held sacred as a chapelle ardente, within whose walls the mother, day after day, spent some solitary hours.

Lady Harriet Cowper had been uncertain and undecided in the form of her religious aspirations. When in Paris, she frequented the Roman Catholic churches in the first days when thought and conscience were busy, meditating there at those times when, but for a few silent figures at prayer, the peaceful gloom was undisturbed. Her impressions deepened after the death of her child; her sympathies took another direction; she em- braced strict evangelical opinions.

She is described at this period by Mrs.

Augustus Craven (Marie Louise de la Ferronays), who saw her at Lady Palmerston's house, Brocket, in Hertfordshire, and who thus depicts her: *—

"Ce ne sera peut-être pas m'écarter ici de mon sujet que d'emprunter encore quelques pages de mon journal d'autrefois, car on y trouvera le portrait d'une femme que sa beauté, son esprit et sa destinée étrange, rendirent jadis célèbre en France, non moins qu'en Angleterre; ce fut chez elle, à la campagne que furent écrites les pages suivants." †

"Novembre, 1856. Je la regardais, ce soir, assise à côté de la grand cheminée du salon; enfoncée dans un grande fauteuil, la tête rejetée en arrière, son visage pâle et régulier tourné de façon à en dessiner l'ovale, si parfait encore, avec cette expression plutôt indolente que calme, et ses belles épaules, à peine couverte d'une légère dentelle. Dans

---

* From an article in the *Correspondent* for February, 1876.

† Brocket Hall had been lent to Mr. Spencer Cowper for a few months.

un temps qui n'est pas encore fort éloigné,
un temps où elle était moins heureuse et
calme qu'aujourd'hui, il m'est souvent arrivé
de voir Lady Harriet dans nos églises.
C'était alors vers les sanctuaires catholiques
qu'elle tournait ses regards, et elle semblait
venir y chercher la paix. Depuis, une nou-
velle ferveur protestante s'est emparée d'elle,
et le mouvement religieux de ses idées a pris
une autre direction." .... "Peu d'années
après que ces pages furent écrites, la belle
Lady Harriet n'existait plus; elle avait achevé
sa vie dans les pratiques d'une piété exem-
plaire, mais dont la forme fut étrange et
s'écarta beaucoup de cette sage loi de l'église
catholique, qui met les devoirs d'état au pre-
mier rang, et veut, selon l'expression de S.
François de Sales, que pour vouloir être de
bons anges nous n'oublions pas d'être de bons
hommes et de bonnes femmes. Lady Harriet quitta, non seulement ses ajustements
splendides, et tout excès de parure et d'élé-
gance, mais elle se revêtit d'un costume

presque religieux, devint sœur d'une sorte de communauté protestante, se livra à des actes extraordinaires de charité, et même à un genre d'apostolat rarement permis aux femmes parmi nous; tout cela cependant sans quitter sa maison, dont elle transforma toutes les habitudes, ni son mari, à qui elle imposa cette transformation. Elle fut sincère, charitable, et courageuse; il ne nous appartient point de juger ses intentions ni de critiquer ses actes."

One or two of the works of charity alluded to—which, although scarcely to be called extraordinary, were more unusual in her day than now, especially carried out, as they were, solely by individual effort and on individual responsibility—may be noticed, and that in particular which was associated with Sandringham.

It was in 1857 that the idea occurred to her of establishing at Sandringham an orphanage for the children of soldiers who had fallen in the Crimean war. A roomy old farmhouse, conveniently near the hall and church, offered

the necessary accommodation; but some difficulties arose as to the after-provision required
in the case of such children, and the scheme
was altered, and adapted to the reception of
orphans without any special qualification. The
orphanage was opened in July, 1858, with
seven young children. Part of the house was
occupied by the village school, part by the
little girls and their matron. They attended
the school every day.

Regularly every morning, during the months
she spent at Sandringham, Lady Harriet
walked to the school at eleven o'clock, taught
for an hour, and then she and Mr. Cowper
took their orphans for a stroll in the park until
their dinner-time, at one o'clock.

Two of them were children taken from one
of the London workhouses, others were born
in Norfolk. Sometimes, during the summer
months, these infants were taken down to the
sea, to bathe and run about in the bright edge
of the water, their little limbs like pink shells
on the sand.

Long after the orphanage had been broken up, the house pulled down, and Lady Harriet had left Sandringham and settled again in Paris, two of these girls were still with her in her house in the Avenue Friedland, where she brought them up with great care, giving them daily instruction until they were grown up.

In Paris she hired a house, and established it as an almshouse for twelve old French women, choosing and arranging the furniture herself for them, with the exception of the covering for their arm-chairs, the colour of which each inmate was to select for herself. The old ladies, like bees—who are said to prefer one colour, blue—had some instinct which invariably led them to choose green. The little wizened Parisians sunned their brown skins in the warm corners of the court where their house stood, long after the death of their benefactress, in 1868, the refuge being retained for them until the last of the twelve had been carried away to her final home.

Lady Harriet Cowper thus mentions the sale of Sandringham :—" The large sum of money obtained (220,000*l.*), and the high station of the purchaser, were great inducements, as we have every reason to hope that the circumstances of the tenantry will be much improved ; but I shall regret the Orphan Home, the Church, the Schools, and the kind, good, grateful people."

The hope, thus expressed, in ignorance of the future, has indeed been amply fulfilled, and larger improvements and advantages than could have been dreamt of in 1861 have justified the choice of this estate for the Prince of Wales's country abode.

Milton Keynes UK
Ingram Content Group UK Ltd.
UKHW022022010124
435322UK00005B/197